Here is your God

Isaiah

by Tim Chester

thegoodbook
COMPANY

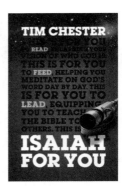

Isaiah For You

If you are reading *Isaiah For You* alongside this Good Book Guide, here is how the studies in this booklet link to the chapters of *Isaiah For You*:

Study One → Ch 1   Study Five → Ch 7
Study Two → Ch 2   Study Six → Ch 8
Study Three → Ch 5   Study Seven → Ch 11
Study Four → Ch 6   Study Eight → Ch 12

Find out more about *Isaiah For You* at:
www.thegoodbook.com/for-you
www.thegoodbook.co.uk/for-you

Here is your God
The Good Book Guide to Isaiah
© Tim Chester, 2021.
Series Consultants: Tim Chester, Tim Thornborough,
                Anne Woodcock, Carl Laferton

Published by:
The Good Book Company

thegoodbook.com | thegoodbook.co.uk
thegoodbook.com.au | thegoodbook.co.nz | thegoodbook.co.in

ISBN: 9781784985608 | Printed in Turkey

CONTENTS

Introduction: Good Book Guides

Every Bible-study group is different—yours may take place in a church building, in a home or in a cafe, on a train, over a leisurely mid-morning coffee or squashed into a 30-minute lunch break. Your group may include new Christians, mature Christians, non-Christians, mums and tots, students, businessmen or teens. That's why we've designed these *Good Book Guides* to be flexible for use in many different situations.

Our aim in each session is to uncover the meaning of a passage, and see how it fits into the ".big picture" of the Bible. But that can never be the end. We also need to appropriately apply what we have discovered to our lives. Let's take a look at what is included:

⊕ **Talkabout:** Most groups need to "break the ice" at the beginning of a session, and here's the question that will do that. It's designed to get people talking around a subject that will be covered in the course of the Bible study.

⊥ **Investigate:** The Bible text for each session is broken up into manageable chunks, with questions that aim to help you understand what the passage is about. The **Leader's Guide** contains **guidance for questions**, and sometimes ⊻ additional "follow-up" questions.

⊡ **Explore more (optional):** These questions will help you connect what you have learned to other parts of the Bible, so you can begin to fit it all together like a jigsaw; or occasionally look at a part of the passage that's not dealt with in detail in the main study.

→ **Apply:** As you go through a Bible study, you'll keep coming across **apply** sections. These are questions to get the group discussing what the Bible teaching means in practice for you and your church. ⊡ **Getting personal** is an opportunity for you to think, plan and pray about the changes that you personally may need to make as a result of what you have learned.

↑ **Pray:** We want to encourage prayer that is rooted in God's word—in line with his concerns, purposes and promises. So each session ends with an opportunity to review the truths and challenges highlighted by the Bible study, and turn them into prayers of request and thanksgiving.

The **Leader's Guide** and introduction provide historical background information, explanations of the Bible texts for each session, ideas for **optional extra** activities, and guidance on how best to help people uncover the truths of God's word.

Why study Isaiah?

Isaiah can seem somewhat intimidating. For one thing it's a big book covering an extended timescale. Sometimes we're immersed in the politics of Isaiah's day; sometimes he's responding to events 100 or so years in the future. It's full of unfamiliar names and places, all set in a very different culture. Large sections may feel like alien territory.

But the book of Isaiah is full of good news and it's news worth shouting about.

Isaiah's ministry begins around 739 BC, "the year that King Uzziah died" (6:1). After an initial "overture" in chapters 1 – 6, we see Isaiah addressing King Ahaz of Judah, inviting him to trust God rather than form an alliance with Assyria (7 – 12). Chapters 13 – 27 contain a series of addresses to various nations, reminding us that the Lord reigns and one day he will restore his reign upon the earth. In 28 – 39 we encounter a different political situation: by now the king is Hezekiah, who reigned 729-686 BC, and the Assyrians have become Judah's greatest threat.

Isaiah also looks beyond his own lifetime, especially in chapters 40 – 66. In 587 BC the Babylonians would defeat Judah and destroy Jerusalem, leading many of its people away into captivity. Isaiah addresses these exiles, promising that God will gather his people home. It's a promise fulfilled in Christ, who leads people from all nations home to a new heavens and a new earth.

The book of Isaiah comforts our fears and sorrows by pointing us to the rest and peace that come from entrusting ourselves to God. It excites us about the church by giving a vision of God's people as a community of justice which brings light to the world. And it fuels our commitment to mission by painting a compelling picture of God gathering people from the four corners of the world.

Most importantly, Isaiah points forward all the time to the coming of Jesus. More than any other Old Testament book, Isaiah forms a bridge between the Old Testament and New.

These eight studies do not look at every part of the book of Isaiah. They are more like a highlights tour—they will help you to understand the shape of the book and see how its main themes work together. As you read it, Isaiah will enlarge your view of God, enrich your love for Christ and sharpen your understanding of salvation. It will provide you with what Isaiah promises in 33:6: a sure foundation for our times.

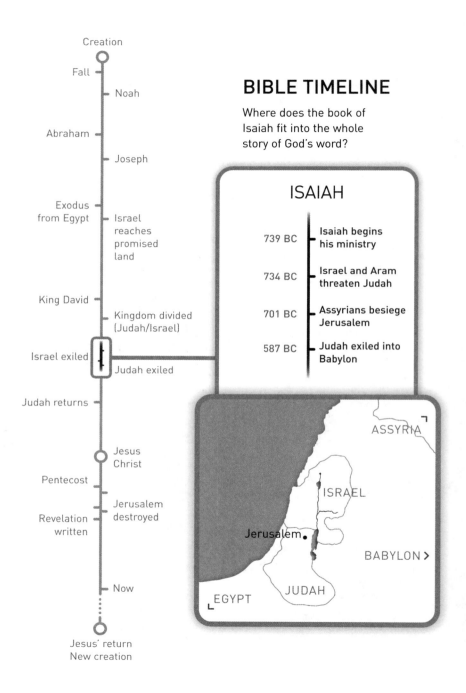

Creation

Fall

Noah

Abraham

Joseph

Exodus
from Egypt

Israel
reaches
promised
land

King David

Kingdom divided
(Judah/Israel)

Israel exiled

Judah exiled

Judah returns

Jesus
Christ

Pentecost

Jerusalem
destroyed

Revelation
written

Now

Jesus' return
New creation

BIBLE TIMELINE

Where does the book of
Isaiah fit into the whole
story of God's word?

ISAIAH

739 BC	Isaiah begins his ministry
734 BC	Israel and Aram threaten Judah
701 BC	Assyrians besiege Jerusalem
587 BC	Judah exiled into Babylon

ASSYRIA

ISRAEL

Jerusalem.

BABYLON >

EGYPT

JUDAH

1

Isaiah 6
HOLY, HOLY, HOLY

⊕ talkabout

1. The American theologian A.W. Tozer once said: "What comes into our minds when we think about God is the most important thing about us". Do you think that's true? Why, or why not?

⊕ investigate

▶ **Read Isaiah 6:1-5**

Isaiah 1 – 5 previews some of the key themes in the book, with warnings of God's judgment on the people's wickedness balanced by expressions of God's love and visions of a glorious future. But Isaiah 6 is the chapter which really defines Isaiah's ministry—which is why we are starting here.

The chapter begins by locating this vision at a particular moment in history. King Uzziah's reign was a golden age of peace and prosperity, but now the winds of change were blowing. Uzziah had died and the Assyrian Empire was like a dark cloud on the horizon.

2. What does Isaiah see in verse 1? What word would you use to sum up this description of God?

3. What else does Isaiah see and hear, in verses 2-4?

• What does this tell us about God?

optional

⊡ explore more

❯ **Read Exodus 19:16-22**

This is another encounter with God. What similarities are there to Isaiah's encounter?

How do you think it felt to encounter God like this?

God's holiness is not so much an attribute of God as it is the perfection and intensity of all his other attributes: his love, power, purity, wisdom and justice. Our God is a consuming fire, burning with the intensity of his holiness like the burning centre of a star. Anything tainted by sin is consumed in the presence of his powerful purity and perfect love. This explains why Isaiah reacts as he does in verse 5.

❯ **Read Isaiah 5:8-30**

4. Who has Isaiah already declared woe to and why?

DICTIONARY

Desolate (v 8): abandoned.
Bath (v 10): about 22 litres.
Homer (v 10): about 160 kilograms.
Ephah (v 10): about 16 kilograms.
Pasture (v 17): field where sheep graze.
Acquit (v 23): declare innocent.
Flint (v 28): a very hard stone.

5. But who does he now declare woe to and why (6:5)?

→ **apply**

6. How does this passage challenge our assumptions about what God is like and what it is like to come into his presence?

⊌ **investigate**

▶ **Read Isaiah 6:6-13**

The coal which the angel touches to Isaiah's lips symbolises the altar—the place of sacrifice, where an animal symbolically took on a person's guilt and died in their place.

7. What happens when the coal touches Isaiah's lips?

DICTIONARY
Live (v 6): burning.
Atoned for (v 7): resolved, forgiven.
Calloused (v 10): rough and hard.
Forsaken (v 12): abandoned.
Terebinth (v 13): a type of tree.

• What links can you spot between this and the way Christ has atoned for his followers' sin?

8. What do you think is going through Isaiah's head as he says, "Here am I. Send me!"?

9. What is Isaiah's job going to be (v 9-10)?

• How will his hearers respond?

10. What is the bad news in verses 11-13?

But there is good news too. The people are not hardened for ever. A "holy seed" will remain: there is the possibility of new growth. It's a theme that re-emerges in Isaiah 11:1, where a shoot will come from the stump of Jesse—the father of King David, Israel's greatest king.

So a chapter that began with the death of one king ends with the promise of another. Out of the wastes of the impending judgment, the promised messianic King will come. Isaiah's ministry is part of this promise. He looks forward to the ultimate coming of Christ.

> **Read Isaiah 52:13-15**

11. Isaiah 52 describes the coming of Jesus. How does verse 15 resolve the problem in Isaiah 6:9-10?

> **DICTIONARY**
>
> **Disfigured, marred (v 14):** damaged.
> **Sprinkle (v 15):** when blood was sprinkled on things, it was a sign that they had been cleansed or become holy.

• What does this tell us about how people come to saving faith?

⊡ apply

12. What things can hold you back from being as willing as Isaiah to obey God's call? How could Isaiah's experience spur you on?

⊡ getting personal

What specific thing might God be calling you to do?

What would it look like to say, "Here am I. Send me?"

⬆ pray

Use the angels' song and Isaiah's responses as a framework for your prayers.

2 Isaiah 8:11 – 9:7
THE PEOPLE WALKING IN DARKNESS

The story so far

Isaiah's ministry began with a vision of the holy God. He saw his own sinfulness, was cleansed, and responded in willingness to speak up for God to his people.

⊕ talkabout

1. What reasons might people have today to see the world as gloomy and dark? How do they try to deal with that perception?

For God's people in Isaiah's time the future looks gloomy. The kingdom of Judah is being threatened by the nations of Aram (or Syria) and Ephraim (or Israel). King Ahaz decides to look for help by doing a deal with another foreign nation, Assyria.

⊕ investigate

▶ Read Isaiah 8:11-22

2. What should the people do in response to these fears about the future of their nation (v 12-17)?

> **DICTIONARY**
>
> **Bind up (v 16):** wrap and tie up.
> **Mount Zion (v 18):** the mountain in Jerusalem on which the temple stood.
> **Mediums and spiritists (v 19):** people who claim to communicate with the dead.
> **Famished (v 21):** starving.

3. What are they tempted to do instead (v 19, 21)?

4. Why doesn't this solve their problems (v 20, 22)?

⊖ apply

5. When are you tempted to "fear what [others] fear" (v 12)? How might this passage change the way you deal with threatening things?

⊕ investigate

❯ Read Isaiah 9:1-5

6. What are the reversals promised in verses 1-2?

DICTIONARY

Zebulun and Naphtali (v 1): two tribes of Israel, whose land was in the northern part of the kingdom.
Galilee (v 1): the northern region of Israel.
Jordan (v 1): a river which flows through the Sea of Galilee.
Midian (v 4): a people defeated by the Israelites under Gideon.

7. What will this involve (v 3-5)?

• How will the people who were in darkness feel now?

☺ **explore more**

optional

optional

☺ **explore more**

Zebulun and Naphtali were the two most northerly of the twelve tribes of Israel (and part of the region of Galilee). So when the Assyrian army came, it came first to Zebulun and Naphtali. The darkness fell on them first.

▶ **Read 1 Kings 9:10-13**

What does this tell us about the towns of Galilee?

How does that affect the way you read Isaiah 9:1-5?

☺ **getting personal**

Reflect on what good news this is. What oppression or war do you long to see an end to? You can pray about it in the knowledge that God has promised an end to those things.

Watch any television news programme or read any newspaper and you will readily see what an amazing promise this is. This is unbelievably good news. But how will God bring it about?

▶ Read Isaiah 9:6-7

8. Look at the political language in these verses. How will this child bring about the changes God has promised?

This is what Isaiah promises and this is what Jesus will deliver. One day Jesus will return to this earth. In the Lord's Prayer we say, "Your kingdom come, your will be done on earth as in heaven." That prayer will be answered when Jesus returns and establishes his government, "upholding it with justice and righteousness from that time on and for ever", as 9:7 says.

⊡ explore more

optional

▶ Read Luke 1:26-33 and Matthew 4:12-13

What links can you spot between these passages and Isaiah 9?

"Wonderful Counsellor" doesn't just mean "a really good counsellor". It's the language of "signs and wonders"—it means Jesus has miraculous or supernatural counsel.

▶ Read Isaiah 11:2-4

9. Where does Jesus' insight come from?

• What does this insight enable him to do?

10. What's the point of calling Jesus "Mighty God" and "Everlasting Father" (9:6)?

⊡ **getting personal**

What conflicts are particularly difficult in your life right now? How does it help to remember that Jesus is the Wonderful Counsellor, Almighty God, Everlasting Father and Prince of Peace?

11. What was the biggest threat to the people in 8:11-22?

• Since that's the background to this passage, what does it mean that Jesus is the Prince of Peace?

⊟ **apply**

12. Isaiah 8:17 says, "I will put my trust in him". How might this passage help you to do this...

• in the face of personal conflict or suffering?

- when people around you are filled with fear about political or social issues?

- when you are struggling with sin or guilt or feeling far from God?

⬆ pray

In what ways do things feel dark at present? Lift those things to God and ask for his help. Try using phrases from today's passage to help you.

Then spend time praising Jesus for who he is. Talk to him about those areas in which the truths in Isaiah 9:6-7 especially need to shape you and your lives.

3 Isaiah 14 and 19:19-25
WHOSE IS THE GLORY?

The story so far

Isaiah's ministry began with a vision of the holy God. He saw his own sinfulness, was cleansed, and responded in willingness to speak up for God to his people.

Against a background of conflict and fear, Isaiah promised light in the darkness. One day God would bring justice and peace through a promised child.

⊕ talkabout

1. How do people perceive the world's political superpowers today? Do they fear them? Hate them? Admire them? Why?

Isaiah 13 – 23 are a collection of prophecies addressed to the nations. The sequence begins with a description of the downfall of the Babylonian empire. Babylon was the regional superpower a hundred years or so after Isaiah's ministry. The Babylonians would destroy Jerusalem, carrying her inhabitants away into exile. But Isaiah is looking forward to the defeat of Babylon two centuries or so later by the Medes and Persians. Ultimately this would lead to the return of the Jews from exile.

⊕ investigate

> Read Isaiah 14:1-23

2. Look at verses 3-6. How did the king of Babylon act?

DICTIONARY

Junipers and cedars (v 8): two types of tree.
Lebanon (v 8): a land to the north of Israel.
Mount Zaphon (v 13): the highest mountain in Syria.

3.   But what will happen to him and to Babylon (v 22-23)?

4.   Look at the different "scenes" used to describe this. What is the key point of each one?
• verses 7-8

• verses 9-11

• verses 12-15

• verses 16-17

• verses 18-21

⊡ **explore more**

The story of the defeat of Babylon is told in Daniel 5.

▶ **Read Daniel 5:1-6, 13-31**

What does Belshazzar do? Is this consistent with Isaiah's portrait of the Babylonian king?

How does Daniel interpret the situation?

⊡ **investigate**

▶ **Read Isaiah 14:24-32**

5. Who else does God's judgment apply to?

• What is the hope given in verse 32?

6. These prophecies were spoken to the people of Judah, not to the nations themselves. How do you think Isaiah wants them to respond?

⤇ apply

7. In what ways do we get sucked into thinking that human glory and status are what matters? Why is this so tempting?

* What attitude should we have instead?

⊡ getting personal

In what ways are you especially tempted to think that status, wealth, beauty or success are what matters? Are you intimidated by anyone who has those things? Do you fear not having them? Do you spend time pursuing them?

How will you use this passage to remind you to put your hope in God alone?

Look back at verse 1. This chapter about the fall of Babylon begins with a focus on the future of God's people. When the Babylonian empire fell, God's people would come home.

The Babylonian exile was a picture of a larger exile—humanity's exile from God. But because of the death and resurrection of Christ, one day God will gather his people and bring us home.

This vision of restoration and welcome becomes positively audacious and outrageous in Isaiah 19, which is a prophecy about Egypt.

⬇ investigate

> **❯ Read Isaiah 19:19-25**

8. Verse 22 says God will strike Egypt with a plague. God did that before the exodus. Egypt is an old enemy. But what is the new and surprising thing that Isaiah adds?

9. How will the Egyptians relate to God when this happens (v 19-21)?

10. What is God's ultimate plan for the Egyptians, Assyrians and Israelites (v 23-25)?

   • How is this a reversal of what we read in Isaiah 14?

❯ Read 2 Corinthians 4:16-18

11. The troubles of human frailty which we saw in Isaiah 14 have not gone away. But what is Paul's perspective on those things?

⊟ apply

12. We often spend time thinking or worrying about the future. How might the passages in today's study change our perspective on this?

⊡ getting personal

How much time do you spend simply "fixing your eyes" on God and his glory? How could you do this more?

⊡ pray

Ask God for help in making Paul's perspective on human frailty your own. Praise him for the glorious future you are promised in Christ and pray for one another about specific ways you can fix your eyes on God's glory instead of human glory.

4 Isaiah 28
GOD'S STRANGE WORK

The story so far

Isaiah's ministry began with a vision of the holy God. He saw his own sinfulness, was cleansed, and responded in willingness to speak up for God to his people.

Against a background of conflict and fear, Isaiah promised light in the darkness. One day God would bring justice and peace through a promised child.

Isaiah predicted the downfall of the Babylonian empire, showing that God's glory and strength is far greater than any fleeting human glory.

⊕ talkabout

1. Have you ever experienced a time when something that was unpleasant or seemed to make no sense was actually used by God for good in some way?

⊕ investigate

❯ Read Isaiah 28:1-29

At this point in history, God's people were divided into two kingdoms. The first part of this chapter is addressed to Israel or Ephraim, the northern kingdom. But it is really designed as a warning to Judah, the southern kingdom. Both are now in danger from the Assyrians.

DICTIONARY

Covenant (v 15): binding agreement.
Plumb-line (v 17): device used for making sure something is straight.
Annulled (v 18): cancelled.
Mount Perazim, Gibeon (v 21): places where David defeated the Philistines.
Caraway, cummin: (v 25): spices.
Barley, spelt (v 25): cereal crops.
Thresh (v 28): beat to separate the edible grain from the useless chaff.

2. In verses 1-4, how does Isaiah express Israel's (or Ephraim's) pride in themselves?

• But why is that pride futile?

3. Verses 7-8 describe some of Israel's leaders. What are they like?

Meanwhile, Isaiah calls the people to turn to God (v 5-6).

4. Verses 9-10 report their response. What do they think of Isaiah's message?

⌨ **getting personal**

Have there been times in your life when God's word just seemed like nonsense? Why? How did you respond? How will you respond in the future?

5. How does God respond to this (v 11-13)?

Israel trusted in their own strength and wisdom, and they ended up being wiped out by Assyria. Isaiah presents this as a warning to the rulers of Judah (v 14). They are now seeking an alliance with Egypt against the threat of Assyria. Like Israel, they are relying on human strength and wisdom instead of on God.

6. In verse 15 Isaiah parodies Judah's claims about its alliance with Egypt. What does he say is really going on?

• What will happen (v 17-19)?

➔ apply

7. This passage functions as a warning to us, too. In what ways are we, even as Christians, tempted to act like Israel or Judah?

• What can we learn from their story?

God is promising destruction. He is going to fight against his people instead of for them (v 21-22). Isaiah calls this God's "strange work" and "alien task". It is not at all what the people want or expect.

But Isaiah has more to say about God's strange work.

8. In verse 24 Isaiah describes the work of a farmer ploughing land. It is a violent process. But what is the farmer's ultimate purpose (v 25)?

• What does that tell us about God's purposes in allowing his people to suffer?

9. In verses 27-28 Isaiah describes someone grinding spices and grain. What do these images suggest about the way God uses suffering?

⊡ **explore more**

optional

❯ **Read Hebrews 12:7-11**

How is hardship described here?

What is God's purpose in this?

So how are we to respond when we suffer?

When we feel overwhelmed by the storms of life, it can feel like everything in which we take refuge is being swept away. It is worth asking ourselves, before this happens, what our confidence is placed in.

What is your hope for life? What is the lie in which you're tempted to take refuge? Do you have a misplaced reliance on human strength or wisdom? What things might God want to strip away from you in order to build you up in greater reliance on him?

10. Back in verses 16-17, God describes a new building project which will stand amid all the destruction. What is it like?

1 Peter 2:4-8 says this cornerstone is Jesus. God destroyed his people and let them be taken into exile so that he could build them afresh. The cornerstone and foundation of the new building is Christ.

11. The ultimate "strange work" of God is the cross. In what ways did that seem destructive? What good things did God bring about through it?

➔ **apply**

12. In what ways are we tempted to "panic" (v 16)—getting in a flap and trying to solve our own problems instead of listening to God?

• What difference will it make to remember that Christ is our cornerstone and that God is building us into a holy people?

⊕ pray

Spend some time praising God, who may work in strange ways but "whose plan is wonderful, whose wisdom is magnificent" (v 29).

Pray for one another. Ask God to use the trials in your life to produce good fruit and to help you to trust him. Here is a quote from Charles Spurgeon which may help you to pray:

"God's people will not be in a hurry to run away, for they shall not be overcome with the fear which causes panic. When others are flying here and there as if their wits had failed them, believers will be quiet, calm, and deliberate. And so they will be able to act wisely in the hour of testing.

"What about me? Am I believing, and am I therefore keeping to the believer's pace, which is walking with God? Be at peace, fluttering spirit! Oh, rest in the Lord, and wait patiently for him!"

(*The Promises of God*, ed. Tim Chester, Crossway, 2019, November 29)

5 Isaiah 37:1 – 38:20
DEFENDING GOD'S HONOUR

The story so far

Isaiah's ministry began with a vision of the holy God. Against a background of conflict and fear, he promised that God would one day bring light and hope.

Isaiah predicted the downfall of the Babylonian empire, showing that God's glory and strength is far greater than any fleeting human glory.

Israel refused to trust God and was destroyed. Isaiah warned the people of Judah to trust God's intentions for them even though they faced destruction.

⊕ talkabout

1. How do you decide if someone is trustworthy?

⊕ investigate

In Isaiah 36 – 39, we turn from prophetic oracle to historical narrative. The Assyrian army has arrived at the gates of Jerusalem. But Hezekiah, the king of Judah, displays magnificent trust in God.

❯ Read Isaiah 37:1-20

2. An Assyrian commander has been speaking to the people. How do Hezekiah (v 4) and God himself, through Isaiah (v 6), evaluate his words?

> **DICTIONARY**
>
> **Blasphemed (v 6):** dishonoured God's name.
> **Lachish, Libnah (v 8):** towns in Judah.
> **Cush (v 9):** a region of North Africa.
> **Gozan, Harran etc (v 12-13):** towns previously destroyed by the Assyrians.

⊡ explore more

Back in Isaiah 36 we see what the commander actually said.

❯ **Read Isaiah 36:4-20**

How does he ridicule and blaspheme God in these speeches?

What does he say to represent Assyria as more powerful than God?

3. What is Sennacherib's argument in verses 10-13?

4. Look at the ways Hezekiah addresses God in verses 16-20. How does he describe God and why are those descriptions relevant to what Sennacherib has just said?

5. What is Hezekiah asking God to do and why?

⊟ apply

6. How often is the glory and reputation of God's name the key issue that is at stake in our own prayers? How would it change our prayers if it were more central?

getting personal

Think of an example of something you have been praying about recently. What would it look like to centre your prayers about that issue or person around the glory and reputation of God?

⊕ **investigate**

▶ **Read Isaiah 37:21-35**

7. What is God's message in...

• verses 22-27?

• verses 28-29?

• verses 30-32?

• verses 33-35?

8. What is the key thing that Sennacherib has done wrong?

What Isaiah promised duly happened. Verses 36-38 tell us that 185,000 Assyrian soldiers mysteriously died. Sennacherib returned home in disgrace and was later assassinated by his sons.

But Hezekiah now meets with fresh disaster: he becomes extremely ill and Isaiah advises him to prepare for death (38:1). Hezekiah, though, prays for deliverance with bitter tears and so God promises to add 15 extra years to his life (v 2-7). In the next section, Hezekiah describes these experiences.

> **Read Isaiah 38:9-20**

9. How does Hezekiah describe what had happened to him (v 10-14)?

• How does God fit into this portrayal?

10. What reasons for his recovery does Hezekiah identify (v 15-20)?

11. What parallels are there between Hezekiah's illness in chapter 38 and the predicament of God's people in chapter 37?

What apparently impossible situations do you or your loved ones face at the moment? Look back at Hezekiah's words throughout Isaiah 37 – 38. What do you find most helpful for your own situation? How could you make his prayers your prayers?

➔ apply

12. How can you get better at trusting and praising God in all situations? Why is this so important?

↑ pray

Use Hezekiah's prayers as a starting point for your own.

6 Isaiah 40
COMFORT MY PEOPLE

The story so far

Isaiah's ministry began with a vision of the holy God. Against a background of conflict and fear, he promised that God would one day bring light and hope.

The downfall of the Babylonians showed that only God is really glorious. Isaiah warned the people of Judah to trust God even though they faced destruction.

King Hezekiah's prayers were full of confidence in who God is. God heard his prayers and saved him both from the Assyrians and from a serious illness.

⊕ talkabout

1. In what situations might people today feel restless and rootless, like exiles?

⬇ investigate

Isaiah wrote in the 8th century BC, but here he looks forward 200 years to the Babylonian exile. The exile of God's people in history was always a pointer to something bigger and deeper, which is humanity's exile from God. Ever since Adam and Eve were expelled from the Garden of Eden, we have lived in exile. So Isaiah 40 is for us all today.

❯ Read Isaiah 40:1-11

2. Isaiah is given a message with which to comfort people. The heart of this message is in verse 9. What is it?

> **DICTIONARY**
>
> **Recompense (v 10):** reward, payment.

• Why might this be comforting—and why might it not be?

3. Verse 10 says that "the Sovereign LORD comes with power". How is this illustrated in verses 3-5?

4. How do the promises in verse 10 contrast with what the exiles have experienced so far (v 2)?

• Why is the time of punishment and exile over, according to verse 2?

5. In verse 11, what does Isaiah say God does when he comes?

6. What did all this mean to those who were in exile in Babylon?

• How was it fulfilled in Jesus' time?

⤷ apply

7. Why is this message still relevant for people today? What might you want to say to people who are...

• feeling guilt and shame?

• facing the consequences of their sin?

• feeling abandoned?

• feeling frail or afraid?

⊡ getting personal

Think about what you have learned in Isaiah so far about what God is like. How might those things link with the concerns and or experiences of particular individuals you know? How could you say to them, in effect, "Here is your God"? Try preparing some sentences you could say to make those links in a conversation.

⊡ investigate

8. As well as being the recipients of this message, we can also put ourselves in the shoes of Isaiah. What does God repeatedly tell him to do?

9. What do verses 6-8 tell us about the nature of God's message?

⊡ explore more

Isaiah 40:6-8 may sound especially familiar. That's because Peter quotes them in 1 Peter.

▶ **Read 1 Peter 1:23-25**

What is the effect of God's word on those who hear and receive it?

▶ **Read Isaiah 40:12-31**

10. What comparisons does Isaiah make in verses 12-26?

• Why are all these comparisons good news for God's people (v 27-31)?

11. Why is all this a motivation to lift up our voices?

→ **apply**

12. How will you lift up your voice in the coming weeks? What will you say and to whom?

⊡ getting personal

Read through Isaiah 40 quietly again. Which of the images do you find most moving or helpful personally? Why? How will you respond?

↑ pray

First use the words of Isaiah 40:12-26 to help you praise God.

Then pray for those you long to respond to the message of the gospel.

7 Isaiah 52:13 – 53:12
THE SUFFERING SERVANT

The story so far

Isaiah's ministry began with a vision of the holy God. Against a background of conflict and fear, he promised that God would one day bring light and hope.

Isaiah predicted the downfall of Babylon and warned the people of Judah to trust God. God saved Jerusalem and King Hezekiah from the Assyrian army.

Looking forward to the exile of Judah, Isaiah described the day when God would come to deliver his people—lifting up his voice to declare God's arrival.

⊕ talkabout

1. Has anyone ever taken your place for something—either in a good way or a bad way? How did it feel?

A key focus of Isaiah 40 – 55 is "the Servant of the LORD" who is introduced in four "songs". Sometimes it seems the Servant is Israel while sometimes the Servant appears to be an individual who redeems Israel. In today's passage the Servant is clearly an individual.

⊕ investigate

> **Read Isaiah 52:13 – 53:12**

2. How do people view the Servant (52:14, 53:1-3)? Why?

DICTIONARY

Transgressions, iniquities (v 5): sins.

3. Why is the Servant punished (v 4-8)? How many different phrases describe this?

• Meanwhile what happens to "us" (v 5)?

4. Imagine a friend or family member were one of the people who "despised" the Servant (53:1-3). What would you say to them?

• Or imagine a friend or family member were one of those who gain peace and healing through the Servant (53:4-5). What would you feel about the Servant's work?

5. Isaiah is looking forward to the coming of Jesus. How was the description of the treatment of the Servant true of Jesus during his lifetime?

• How is it still true of him today?

God passed sentence on our sin and that sentence was borne by Christ. The theological term for this is "penal substitution" ("penal" as in "penalty"). It means paying the penalty of sin in the place of another. Jesus endured the judicial wrath of God in our place.

God's attributes cannot be played off one against another. He cannot stop being holy so he can show mercy. He cannot suspend his justice to extend forgiveness to his people. But through the substitutionary death of his Son, God is true to every aspect of his character—showing mercy while remaining just.

⊡ explore more

optional

In these words the Spirit reveals how our salvation would be achieved. But it didn't come out of the blue. It was not without precedent. Isaiah had many pictures and parallels to connect it to. One is found in Leviticus 16, which describes how God instituted an annual festival in which atonement was made for the sins of the people.

▶ Read Leviticus 16:15-16, 20-22

What is the substitution here?

How do these goats point towards Jesus?

⊡ apply

6. How do we usually respond when we ourselves are rejected? How might this passage alter our perspective?

⊡ getting personal

Think back to a time when you rejected Jesus. Perhaps it was before you became a Christian. Perhaps it was a time when you refused to obey him. Try using the words of this passage to articulate why you did that, and why it was so important to turn to Christ in repentance. Then, could you turn that into an explanation of why you follow Jesus for a non-Christian friend?

⊡ investigate

7. How does the Servant behave through his suffering (v 7, 9)?

8. What happens to the Servant after he has suffered (v 10-12)? Why?

9. What is the result for sinners?

The death of Christ was the centrepiece of a divine plan stretching beyond time into eternity. The Son covenanted to offer himself as a sacrifice for our sins and the Father covenanted to accept that sacrifice. "It was the LORD's will to crush him" (v 10) yet it was also Jesus himself who "poured out his life" and willingly "bore the sin of many" (v 12).

10. Why is the willing participation of Jesus important to our understanding of the cross?

11. Look back at 52:15. How will the nations respond?

• How do we see this promise being fulfilled today?

⊡ explore more

Back in Isaiah 6, Isaiah felt he was being "ruined" (literally "crushed") by the holiness of God. But he was not crushed. Instead Jesus was crushed on his behalf (53:5, 10).

❯ Read Isaiah 57:15

How does this verse remind you of the description of God in Isaiah 6?

When we feel crushed by a sense of sin, how does this verse help?

⊡ getting personal

Write out or read aloud the passage with your own name in the place of "mankind" and "our" et cetera.

For example: *He was despised and rejected by _____ ... Surely he took up _____'s sorrows.*

How does this challenge you? How does it encourage you?

⊖ apply

12. What attitude towards our own sin does Isaiah 52:13 – 53:12 teach us to have?

• What difference should that make to us day to day?

⬆ pray

Confess your sin and use the words of Isaiah to tell one another that you are forgiven. Spend some time praising God for this.

8 Isaiah 60
LIGHT TO THE WORLD

The story so far

Isaiah's ministry began with a vision of the holy God. Against a background of conflict and fear, he promised that God would one day bring light and hope.

Isaiah predicted the downfall of Babylon and warned the people of Judah to trust God. God saved Jerusalem and King Hezekiah from the Assyrian army.

Isaiah described the day when God would come to deliver his people. He predicted a Servant who would suffer on behalf of many and free us from guilt.

⊕ talkabout

1. In what specific ways does the world seem dark at the moment? What might it look like for light to shine?

⊌ investigate

❯ Read Isaiah 8:21-22; 9:1-3; 42:5-7; 49:6; 53:11

2. What do darkness and light represent in each of these verses?

> **DICTIONARY**
>
> **Jacob (49:6):** here, a term for the Israelites.
> **Gentiles (49:6):** non-Jews.

> **Read Isaiah 60:1-9**

3. What do you think verses 1-2 are talking about? What is Isaiah predicting?

4. The light shines—but who else does (v 1, 5)?

In John 8:12, Jesus says, "I am the light of the world". But in Matthew 5:14 he says, "You are the light of the world".

> **Read Matthew 5:14-16**

5. What is Jesus calling us to do in these verses, and why?

6. Back in Isaiah 60:3-9, what is the result of the shining of the people?

• What does this point to in the modern day?

⊙ apply

7. What can your church do to radiate the light of Christ in your community? What roles do good deeds have in the mission of the church?

⊡ getting personal

In the knowledge that it is God's light you are reflecting, identify one specific step you could take this week to shine more brightly for Jesus...

• through your words.

• through your actions.

⊙ investigate

❯ Read Isaiah 60:10-22

8. These verses describe a restored Jerusalem. Where will the beauty and wealth of the new city come from (v 10-14)?

> **DICTIONARY**
>
> **Triumphal procession (v 11):** victory parade featuring captured enemies.
> **Perish (v 12):** die.
> **Juniper, fir, cypress (v 13):** three types of tree.

9. Who will be the ultimate source of glory (v 13, 19-20)?

Isaiah's vision is moving beyond this world and into the next world. His description of the restored Jerusalem is no longer about the physical city and the return from exile which happened in history. He sees far into the future. The new Jerusalem is still in the future even for us today.

🔅 explore more

optional

The kings of the earth had brought their splendour to Jerusalem before Isaiah's time, during Solomon's reign.

▶ **Read 1 Kings 4:20-21 and 5:1-12**

Where did Solomon's wealth come from?

What was it used for?

What parallels can you find in Isaiah 60?

▶ **Read Revelation 21:23-26**

DICTIONARY

The Lamb (v 23): Jesus.

10. In this passage, John describes his vision of the new Jerusalem. What parallels can you find between this passage and Isaiah 60?

➡ apply

11. John's vision in Revelation is a vision of the future. What will be the end result of the light we bring to our dark world?

• Practically speaking, what can you do to reach different groups—whether in your community or further afield?

12. Read through Isaiah 60 again. What do you find most encouraging? What will this passage spur you on to do?

13. In our first study we read about a vision of God which defined Isaiah's ministry. How have these studies changed or enlarged your own view of God? What impact will you allow that to have on your life—and in what ways?

⬆ **pray**

Use your answers to Q12 and Q13 to pray for one another.

Here is your God
LEADER'S GUIDE

Leader's Guide to Isaiah

INTRODUCTION

Leading a Bible study can be a bit like herding cats—everyone has a different idea of what the passage could be about, and a different line of enquiry that they want to pursue. But a good group leader is more than someone who just referees this kind of discussion. You will want to:

- correctly understand and handle the Bible passage. But also...

- encourage and train the people in your group to do this for themselves. Don't fall into the trap of spoon-feeding people by simply passing on the information in the Leader's Guide. Then...

- make sure that no Bible study is finished without everyone knowing how the passage is relevant for them. What changes do you all need to make in the light of the things you have been learning? And finally...

- encourage the group to turn all that has been learned and discussed into prayer.

Your Bible-study group is unique, and you are likely to know better than anyone the capabilities, backgrounds and circumstances of the people you are leading. That's why we've designed these guides with a number of optional features. If they're a quiet bunch, you might want to spend longer on *talkabout*. If your time is limited, you can choose to skip *explore more*, or get people to look at these questions at home. Can't get enough of Bible study? Well, some studies have optional extra homework projects. As leader, you can adapt and select the material to the needs of your particular group.

So what's in the Leader's Guide? The main thing that this Leader's Guide will help you to do is to understand the major teaching points in the passage you are studying, and how to apply them. As well as guidance for the questions, the Leader's Guide for each session contains the following important sections:

THE BIG IDEA

One or two key sentences will give you the main point of the session. This is what you should be aiming to have fixed in people's minds as they leave the Bible study. And it's the point you need to head back toward when the discussion goes off at a tangent.

SUMMARY

An overview of the passage, including plenty of useful historical background information.

OPTIONAL EXTRA

Usually this is an introductory activity that ties in with the main theme of the Bible study, and is designed to "break the ice" at the beginning of a session. Or it may be a "homework project" that people can tackle during the week.

So let's take a look at the various different features of a Good Book Guide:

⊕ talkabout

Each session kicks off with a discussion question, based on the group's opinions or experiences. It's designed to get people talking and thinking in a general way about the main subject of the Bible study.

⬇ investigate

The first thing you and your group need to know is what the Bible passage is about, which is the purpose of these questions. But watch out—people may come up with answers based on their experiences or teaching they have heard in the past, without referring to the passage at all. It's amazing how often we can get through a Bible study without actually looking at the Bible! If you're stuck for an answer, the Leader's Guide contains guidance for questions. These are the answers to direct your group to. This information isn't meant to be read out to people—ideally, you want them to discover these answers from the Bible for themselves. Sometimes there are optional follow-up questions (see ⊻ in guidance for questions) to help you help your group get to the answer.

⊡ explore more

These questions generally point people to other relevant parts of the Bible. They are useful for helping your group to see how the passage fits into the "big picture" of the whole Bible. These sections are OPTIONAL—only use them if you have time. Remember that it's better to finish in good time having really grasped one big thing from the passage, than to try and cram everything in.

⮕ apply

We want to encourage you to spend more time working at application—too often, it is simply tacked on at the end. In the Good Book Guides, apply sections are mixed in with the investigate sections of the study. We hope that people will realize that application is not just an optional extra, but rather, the whole purpose of studying the

Bible. We do Bible study so that our lives can be changed by what we hear from God's word. If you skip the application, the Bible study hasn't achieved its purpose.

These questions draw out practical lessons that we can all learn from the Bible passage. You can review what has been learned so far, and think about practical differences that this should make in our churches and our lives. The group gets the opportunity to talk about what they personally have learned.

⊡ getting personal

These can be done at home, but it is well worth allowing a few moments of quiet reflection during the study for each person to think and pray about specific changes they need to make in their own lives. Why not have a time for reporting back at the beginning of the following session, so that everyone can be encouraged and challenged by one another to make application a priority?

⬆ pray

In Acts 4:25-30 the first Christians quoted Psalm 2 as they prayed in response to the persecution of the apostles by the Jewish religious leaders. Today however, it's not as common for Christians to base prayers on the truths of God's word as it once was. As a result, our prayers tend to be weak, superficial and self-centred rather than bold, visionary and God-centred.

The prayer section is based on what has been learned from the Bible passage. How different our prayer times would be if we were genuinely responding to what God has said to us through his word.

1 Isaiah 6:1-13
HOLY, HOLY, HOLY

THE BIG IDEA
God is holy. When we grasp this we gain a truer view of our sinful souls. We confess our sins, find cleansing and respond in willingness to serve.

SUMMARY
Isaiah 6 describes a vision of God that became the defining perspective of Isaiah's life and ministry.

In verses 1-4, Isaiah sees the reality of God's holiness in the wings of the angels, which cover their eyes and feet in God's presence. This is matched by what he hears from their lips: "Holy, holy, holy is the LORD Almighty". He feels the holiness of God as the doorposts shake and he smells the holiness of God as smoke fills the temple.

God's holiness is not so much an attribute of God as it is the perfection and intensity of all his other attributes. Our God is a consuming fire, burning with the intensity of his holiness. Anything tainted by sin is consumed.

Previously Isaiah declared woe on other people, but now he cries out: "Woe to me! ... I am ruined!" (v 5). Isaiah knows he is a sinner. So are we. If we think we're basically ok, we've not grasped the terrifying holiness and majesty of God.

But God can take away our guilt. For Isaiah that means a coal from the altar. The coal touches his lips and cleanses him from sin (v 7).

When you've seen the majesty of God and when you've experienced his grace, you cannot help but serve him. So Isaiah says, "Send me!" (v 8). But the job that Isaiah gets is not a great one: he's to speak to people who will refuse to listen (v 9-10)!

However, the people are not hardened for ever. Isaiah 6 ends with the words, "The holy seed will be the stump in the land" (v 13). It's a theme that re-emerges in Isaiah 11:1, where a shoot will come from the stump of Jesse—the father of King David. In other words, out of the wastes of judgment, the promised King will come.

Isaiah will encounter people who hear but do not understand. But we read in Isaiah 52:15 that one day there will be people who have not heard but do understand. God is talking about us. We were deaf to God's voice and blind to his glory, but in Christ, God sought us out.

What are we to do in response to this vision of God's holiness? First, we open our eyes to the holiness of God and cry out in humility, asking for cleansing. Second, we take our own holiness seriously. We need to be ruthless with sin and flee temptation. We need to hear the call to service and respond as Isaiah did, "Here am I. Send me!"

OPTIONAL EXTRA
Find a video of Queen Elizabeth II of England's coronation in 1953. Watch the part where she processes through the cathedral with attendants holding her robe, then the response when she is actually crowned. This is a good preparation for thinking about the splendour and majesty of God, as we will do in today's session.

GUIDANCE FOR QUESTIONS

1. The American theologian A.W. Tozer once said: "What comes into our minds when we think about God is the most important thing about us". Do you think that's true? Why, or why not? To get a discussion going, encourage the group to think about some different perspectives people may have about God and how that alters the way they see themselves and others or the way they act. Tozer went on to explain, "We tend by a secret law of the soul to move toward our mental image of God". In other words, our danger is to think of God simply as a bigger or better version of ourselves. We assume God is like us, but with more power or greater moral consistency. We think of ourselves first and then make God in our likeness. That's the wrong way round!

2. What does Isaiah see in verse 1? What word would you use to sum up this description of God? This verse is a royal description. God is first introduced as "the Lord". This describes his role as the Sovereign who rules the earth. He is also "high and exalted". Even today we talk about "your royal highness" and monarchs "ascend" to the throne. Here in Isaiah's vision the Lord is physically above everyone else to show the supremacy of his power. So, good words to sum up this description are "king", "royal" or "supreme".

3. What else does Isaiah see and hear, in verses 2-4? Isaiah sees seraphim, which are angelic beings, made by God to attend him in his heavenly court. They have six wings, two for moving around and four for covering their eyes and feet in God's presence. He hears their song as they fly around. Then to complete the full sensory

experience he feels the doorposts shake and smells smoke filling the temple.

- **What does this tell us about God?**
  - The seraphim have to cover themselves in God's presence. These are beings which have never sinned. You might think that puts them on a moral par with God. But not sinning is just the negative. What God also possesses are the positive attributes of holiness and purity. And he possesses them with such intensity that the seraphim, even though they have never sinned, must expend two-thirds of their energy simply on protecting themselves from God's holiness.
  - This reality is matched by what they sing. The repetition of words in Hebrew is a way of emphasising something. So the angels are saying that God is the holiest of holiest of holy beings.

EXPLORE MORE
Read Exodus 19:16-22. This is another encounter with God. What similarities are there to Isaiah's encounter? There is smoke and trembling (v 18), alongside several other dramatic sights and sounds. Once again God is far above the people, this time on the top of the mountain. God's holiness is represented not by the angels' song but by the cloud of smoke which shielded the people from the sight of God's glory.

How do you think it felt to encounter God like this? The scene at Mount Sinai Is terrifying. Perhaps it was even more so for Isaiah. Instead of being at a distance, he was right in the middle of all this noise and smoke. And in his mind must surely have been the words "the Lord will break out against them" (Exodus 19:22).

**4. Who has Isaiah already declared woe

to and why?

- v 8-10: "Woe to you who add house to house".
- v 11-17: "Woe to those who rise early … to run after their drinks".
- v 18-19: "Woe to those who draw sin along with cords of deceit".
- v 20: "Woe to those who call evil good and good evil".
- v 21: "Woe to those who are wise in their own eyes".
- v 22-30: "Woe to those who are heroes at drinking wine".

All these people are wicked in one way or another. They have turned away from God and are living selfishly. Isaiah declares woe to them because their future is ruin. The Lord is angry with them (v 25).

5. But who does he now declare woe to and why (6:5)? The seventh woe Isaiah declares against himself. "Woe to you" becomes "woe to me". Isaiah feels totally crushed by God's holiness as he recognises his own sin, calling himself "a man of unclean lips". Remember, Isaiah was gifted by God and called by God to speak God's word with his lips. The main way he served God was with his lips. Yet when he sees God's holiness he recognises that even his service of God is tainted by sin.

6. APPLY: How does this passage challenge our assumptions about what God is like and what it is like to come into his presence? As Christians we are in a different position from Isaiah. Because of Christ we are able to come into God's presence boldly (Hebrews 4:16; 10:19). But that does not mean that we should think of it as a light or easy thing. This passage shows that the holiness of God is a threat to sinful people. By nature we are condemned by our sin. So if you

think you're basically ok before God, you've not grasped the terrifying holiness and majesty of God. As Christians we know the presence of God's Spirit within us now, and one day we will see him face to face. But we should never take this reality for granted.

7. What happens when the coal touches Isaiah's lips? God takes away Isaiah's guilt. The coal, being from the altar, symbolises the idea that Isaiah's punishment has been taken by someone else.

- **What links can you spot between this and the way Christ has atoned for his followers' sin?** There is a link between the altar which the coal comes from and the cross on which Jesus died. Jesus is the perfect sacrifice, who takes away the sin of the world. Another link is that Isaiah has done nothing to deserve mercy from God. It is freely given—just as Jesus' atoning blood was freely given for us.

8. What do you think is going through Isaiah's head as he says, "Here am I. Send me!"? He cannot be thinking, "I'll do you a favour" or "I'm the ideal man for the job". He's just said, "I am a man of unclean lips"! But he has seen the majesty of God and experienced his grace. So he cannot help but serve God.

9. What is Isaiah's job going to be (v 9-10)? The job that Isaiah gets is not a great one: he's to speak to people who will refuse to listen! In fact, he's going to make the situation worse, because…

- **How will his hearers respond?** … the more Isaiah speaks, the more opposed to God people will become. God is going to use Isaiah to harden their hearts, confirm their blindness and prepare them for judgment.

**10. What is the bad news in verses
11-13?** Isaiah asks, "For how long, Lord?"
in 6:11 and is told it will be until "the cities
lie ruined'; that is, until Israel and Judah
have been defeated and exiled.
But there is good news too. The people
are not hardened for ever. A "holy seed"
will remain: there is the possibility of new
growth. It's a theme that re-emerges in
Isaiah 11:1, where a shoot will come from
the stump of Jesse—the father of King
David, Israel's greatest king. So a chapter
that began with the death of one king ends
with the promise of another. Out of the
wastes of the impending judgment, the
promised messianic King will come. Isaiah's
ministry is part of this promise. He looks
forward to the ultimate coming of Christ.

**11. Isaiah 52 describes the coming of
Jesus. How does verse 15 resolve the
problem in Isaiah 6:9-10?** 52:15 is the
exact opposite of 6:9. Isaiah will encounter
people who hear, but do not understand.
But one day there will be people who have
not heard, but do understand. (We find
the same idea in 65:1 where God says, "I
revealed myself to those who did not ask
for me; I was found by those who did not
seek me.")

• **What does this tell us about how
people come to saving faith?** God is
the one who saves people—it's all his
decision. Even if you can remember a
period when you were searching for God,
it's because God himself put that longing
in your heart. In his grace he sought you
out. By nature, we are deaf to God's voice
and blind to his glory (6:9-10). Even those
who encountered the glory of God in the
person of Christ were blind to that glory
(John 12:37-41, quoting Isaiah 6:10 and

53:1). But the Holy Spirit opens our ears
and eyes to recognise the glory of God in
the face of Jesus Christ.

**12. APPLY: What things can hold you
back from being as willing as Isaiah
to obey God's call? How could Isaiah's
experience spur you on?**
• We may feel we are too sinful and cannot
be used by God. But Isaiah too was sinful
and God still used him. In Christ we
can have confidence that we have been
forgiven and cleansed and that God is at
work in us.
• Conversely, we may have too high a view
of ourselves, which can lead us to be
complacent about the way we are serving
God. Only when we humble ourselves
before God will we have a proper view of
things. We owe everything to him so we
should give everything.
• We may be afraid of how people
will respond. But we can see from
Isaiah's example that ultimately this is
down to God. We should persevere in
telling people about Jesus and not be
dejected about bad results—after all,
they probably will not be as bad as the
response Isaiah saw!

2 Isaiah 8:11 – 9:7
THE PEOPLE WALKING IN DARKNESS

THE BIG IDEA

God promises light in darkness—the hope of justice and peace in a world of conflict and fear. Ultimately, he brings an end to our conflict with himself. So when the world seems dark, we should remember that God is far greater than any threat, and put our trust in him.

SUMMARY

For God's people the future looks gloomy. The kingdom of Judah is being threatened by neighbouring peoples. King Ahaz has decided to look for help by doing a deal with another foreign nation, Assyria.

Isaiah says that it's not political plots and conspiracies that we should fear, but the Lord (8:11-17). Yet the people reject God. Some consult mediums and spiritists (v 19). They don't want to hear Isaiah's "testimony of warning" (v 20). They prefer to look elsewhere. Others blame God (v 21). But the result is that they look outwards and see only gloom (v 22).

This is the dark backdrop to the wonderful promises of Isaiah 9:1-7. "A light has dawned" (v 2). Gloom will be replaced by joy.

Why? God is going to end oppression and war (v 4-5). Verses 6-7 explain how: "For to us a child is born". This is not a description of a cute, harmless baby. These verses are full of political language. It's the promise of a new and better government. The burden of debt will be lifted. The gloom of unemployment will end. The fear of sexual harassment will be gone. The threat of conflict will disappear.

This is what Isaiah promises—and this is what Jesus will deliver.

King Jesus will be a "Wonderful Counsellor" (v 6). This means that he has miraculous or supernatural counsel. Isaiah elaborates on this in 11:2-4, where it is clear that Jesus has Spirit-enabled insight. He is also the "Mighty God" and "Everlasting Father". In Christ, God enters our world to sort it out. His people are born again as a new people.

And he is "Prince of Peace". This is not just about ending human conflict. We need to read Isaiah's promise in chapter 9 in the light of his warning in 8:12-13: "The Lord Almighty ... is the one you are to fear". Behind all the machinations of ancient geopolitics, God was judging the nations. This was a pointer to the judgment facing all humanity. The day is coming when we will all face God. That's our real problem.

But we can be reconciled with God and live at peace with him through Christ. Today we look forward to the coming reign of Jesus. We need to say, "I will put my trust in him" (8:17).

OPTIONAL EXTRA

Find some adverts or posters from the time of the Second World War (or choose a more recent time such as the coronavirus pandemic) and print them (or ask each group member to bring one). Give one to each person and ask them to present its message to the group. What was the "darkness" or difficulty identified in it? What was the "light" or hope promised?

GUIDANCE FOR QUESTIONS

1. What reasons might people have today to see the world as gloomy and dark? How do they try to deal with that perception? Perhaps the group may bring up global issues such as climate change, the coronavirus pandemic or shifting geopolitical power. Alternatively there may be personal issues such as health problems or financial worries. People deal with these things in many different ways, from pretending they aren't happening to proactively campaigning for change or demanding help. They may seek refuge in leisure time or other distractions. Or they may find themselves taking their anger out on their friends and family members!

2. What should the people do in response to these fears about the future of their nation (v 12-17)? It is not political plots and conspiracies that they should fear but the Lord (v 12-13). This is because, as we saw in Isaiah 6, it is God's holiness that threatens our ruin (v 14-15). So instead of doing a deal with Assyria, the people of Judah should "wait for the Lord" and trust in his help (v 17). If he is the main threat against them, he is also their only hope.

3. What are they tempted to do instead (v 19, 21)?
- v 19: Some take what we might call the superstitious option. They go to mediums for guidance about this life or reassurance about the life to come.
- v 21: Others blame God for what has happened. The equivalent today would be

to say, "If God is so loving, why does he allow suffering?"

4. Why doesn't this solve their problems (v 20, 22)?
- v 20: Mediums claim to consult the dead, but those are the people who have lost the battle with our biggest threat—death itself! By definition they're clearly not the best people to consult. Indeed, Isaiah says, "they have no light of dawn".
- v 22: In verse 21 they look upwards and curse God; now they look outwards and see only gloom. That's what happens when you take God out of the picture. There's no light of revelation and no hope for redemption. Humanity is left to itself and that is not a happy prospect.

5. APPLY: When are you tempted to "fear what [others] fear" (v 12)? How might this passage change the way you deal with threatening things? Encourage the group to think back to their answers to Q1. In the end this passage should help us to put our trust in the Lord even when fearful things are happening around us. It may be tempting to fear political plots or conspiracies, but the Lord is far greater than those things and his holiness far more important. It may be tempting to adopt superstitions or use other means of guidance to get us through life, but those things are limited (at best): they offer no solution to the ultimate problem of death. It may be tempting to curse God or try to do without him, but without God there is only distress and gloom. So whatever happens, we need to put our trust in him.

6. What are the reversals promised in verses 1-2?
- These lands have been humbled, but now they will be honoured.

- The distress, darkness and gloom with which we ended chapter 8 are going to give way to light.

7. What will this involve (v 3-5)?
- God is going to end oppression: he will shatter "the yoke that burdens them" (v 4). All the injustice, exploitation, insecurity, unfair wages and corruption that scar our world will be eradicated.
- God is going to end war: "every warrior's boot" will be burned (v 5).
- **How will the people who were in darkness feel now?** Gloom will be replaced by joy. Verse 3 talks about joy four times. The people will rejoice "as people rejoice at the harvest", because oppression will cease and they will enjoy the fruits of their labour. And they will rejoice like "warriors ... dividing the plunder", because war will be at an end.

EXPLORE MORE
Read 1 Kings 9:10-13. What does this tell us about the towns of Galilee? 20 Galilean towns had been given to Hiram king of Tyre by Solomon in return for building supplies, but it seems Hiram had been somewhat underwhelmed by what he had received. He nicknamed them "the Land of Kabul" which means "good-for-nothing". No wonder Isaiah says they were humbled.
How does that affect the way you read Isaiah 9:1-5? Knowing the background of the towns of Galilee emphasises the reversals in these verses.

8. Look at the political language in these verses. How will this child bring about the changes God has promised?
Isaiah promises a royal child who will end oppression and war. Instead of oppression, he will establish and uphold his kingdom

with justice (9:7b). Instead of war, his government will bring a peace to which "there will be no end" (9:7a).

EXPLORE MORE
Read Luke 1:26-33 and Matthew 4:12-14. What links can you spot between these passages and Isaiah 9?
- Luke 1:26-27: Nazareth is a town in Galilee—the place where Isaiah 9:1-2 said light will dawn. The virgin is married to a descendant of David—just as Isaiah 9:7 had promised.
- Luke 1:31-33: Isaiah 7:14 says "The virgin will conceive"; the angel says, "You will conceive". Isaiah 9:6 says, "A child is born ... a son is given"; the angel says Mary "will give birth to a son". Isaiah 9:7 says, "He will reign on David's throne"; the angel says, "The Lord God will give him the throne of his father David". Isaiah 9:7 says, "He will reign ... over his kingdom ... for ever"; the angel says, "He will reign over Jacob's descendants for ever; his kingdom will never end".
- Matthew makes the same geographical link. The early ministry of Jesus took place in Galilee. This was where the light first dawned, just as Isaiah said it would. But, of course, the real point Matthew is making is that Jesus is the light. He is the one who ends our fear and dispels our gloom.

9. Where does Jesus' insight come from? The insight of Jesus comes from the Spirit of the Lord.

- **What does this insight enable him to do?** The insight of Jesus gives him wisdom, understanding, counsel, might, and the knowledge and fear of the Lord. As a result, his decisions are just and his reign is righteous.

10. What's the point of calling Jesus "Mighty God" and "Everlasting Father" (9:6)?

- Isaiah says "a child is born". This is undoubtedly a human being with a human origin. And yet he's also the Mighty God. Isaiah uses the same phrase in 10:21 to describe how God saves the remnant of his people. God has got involved in our broken world. He didn't look down from above, muttering about the mess we were making of his world. He rolled up his sleeves and got stuck in. God has entered our world to sort it out.

- "Everlasting Father" looks like an odd description, especially as the coming king has just been called "a child" and "a son". But the point is that God has been a father to his people. He created them, reared them and cared for them. And now the king is coming to re-create God's people. They are going to be born again as a new people.

11. What was the biggest threat to the people in 8:11-22? The conflict between humans and God. Behind all the machinations of ancient geopolitics, God was judging the nations. What happened to these nations nearly three millennia ago was a sign and pointer to the judgment facing all humanity. God is holy, and that threatens our ruin.

- **Since that's the background to this passage, what does it mean that Jesus is the Prince of Peace?** At the birth of Jesus, the angels sang, "Glory to God in the highest heaven, and on earth peace to those on whom his favour rests" (Luke 2:14). They were not simply declaring the end of human conflict. They were declaring peace with God. The God we have made our enemy was coming to earth to offer peace to all who would

receive it. He came in the person of his Son to die in our place, making reparation for the wrongs we have done.

12. APPLY: Isaiah 8:17 says, "I will put my trust in him". How might this passage help you to do this...

- **in the face of personal conflict or suffering?** Even when we are filled with pain or fear, we can depend on the fact that we can know Jesus as our Wonderful Counsellor, Mighty God, Everlasting Father and Prince of Peace. We can also look forward to the coming reign of Jesus. When we do so, our gloomy future becomes a bright future.

- **when people around you are filled with fear about political or social issues?** People become worried about crime or war or other issues. Many of these are real threats—but we don't need to get caught up in these fears, because the point is they're not our ultimate threat. Our real problem is that we will one day all face God, and "he is the one you are to fear" (v 13). Yet God has made peace with us through Christ. So we don't need to be overwhelmed by fear of anything in this life.

- **when you are struggling with sin or guilt or feeling far from God?** Through Christ, the Prince of Peace, we are reconciled with God and live at peace with him. We no longer need to be afraid.

3 Isaiah 14 and 19:19-25
WHOSE IS THE GLORY?

THE BIG IDEA

God is more glorious than any power. Success, wealth and other forms of human glory will not last. Instead of chasing them, we, including people from every nation, must humble ourselves before him.

SUMMARY

Isaiah 13 – 23 are a collection of prophecies addressed to the nations. The sequence begins with Babylon. A hundred years or so after Isaiah's ministry, the Babylonians would destroy Jerusalem, carrying her inhabitants away into exile. But Isaiah is looking forward to the defeat of Babylon two centuries or so later.

Isaiah gives God's people a taunt to sing when Babylon oppression comes to an end (14:3-4). He uses a series of "scenes" to describe the fall of Babylon and its king. The point is this: no matter how far your star rises, no matter how high you climb, in the end "you are brought down ... to the depths of the pit" (v 15). There is a complete reversal. Every great king becomes a dead king, and every mighty man becomes a weak man. Throughout history people have conspired and fought to gain power. And every single one of them loses that power when they die. We do it now as much as ever—in nations, in workplaces, in homes. We get sucked into thinking that human glory and status are what matters. But in the end everyone comes to nothing.

In verse 26 Isaiah says, "This is the plan determined for the whole world; this is the hand stretched out over all nations". In other words, Babylon's judgment is a pointer to the judgment of all humanity.

But there is a refuge from God's judgment: "Zion" (v 32). Zion was the hill upon which Jerusalem was built. But Isaiah is not talking about physical Jerusalem. He is talking about the people of God, the faithful remnant, those who find refuge in Jesus Christ.

This vision of restoration and welcome becomes positively audacious and outrageous in 19:19-25. The Egyptians are old oppressors of Israel, but now it's they who will cry out to the Lord and it's to them that God will send a saviour. Egypt are going to acknowledge God and worship him. This is God's grace!

In 2 Corinthians 3:18 Paul reminds us that we "are being transformed into [the Lord's] image with ever-increasing glory". Here is a glory that we do not have to earn or create. We simply look into the face of Christ. Human glory is temporary and fleeting, but God leads us into eternal glory.

OPTIONAL EXTRA

Ask everyone to share something about a place in the world they'd like to visit and why. What is impressive or attractive about that place or that culture? Alternatively, turn this into a game. Choose 8 holiday destinations and find out how much it costs to travel to each one. Split the group into two, give each group a list of the destinations and ask them to guess the prices by putting them in order of most expensive to least expensive. The most accurate group wins. Next, ask the groups to rank the places in order of how much they'd like to go there. This should cause some debate! Again, the point is to think about what we regard as impressive or valuable. Do we pursue wealth, luxury, beauty, human relationships—or something else?

GUIDANCE FOR QUESTIONS

1. How do people perceive the world's political superpowers today? Do they fear them? Hate them? Admire them? Why? This question is designed to get the group talking and help them to make the link between themselves and the people of God in this passage, who are facing threats from other nations.

2. Look at verses 3-6. How did the king of Babylon act?
- v 3-4: he was an oppressor, who forced harsh labour on the Jews.
- v 5-6: he was a wicked ruler who pursued war and aggression against many nations.

3. But what will happen to him and to Babylon (v 22-23)? He will be brought down and defeated. Babylon's oppression will end entirely.

4. Look at the different "scenes" used to describe this. What is the key point of each one?
- **v 7-8:** The defeat of Babylon is a joyful moment for the land, which has a rest from war.
- **v 9-11:** The king will die like everyone else. All his wealth and power will have been for nothing.
- **v 12-15:** The king is pictured as a star. He has "reached for the stars"—trying to raise himself into a place of glory and even making divine claims (v 14). But he

will fall to rock bottom: the very "depths of the pit" (v 15).
- **v 16-17:** The king's success is turned upside down. The king who overthrew nations will be overthrown, and people will taunt him instead of fearing him.
- **v 18-21:** The king will not even be properly buried, and his children will not survive. He will not take his wealth to the grave, and no one will inherit it.

EXPLORE MORE
Read Daniel 5:1-6, 13-31. What does Belshazzar do? Is this consistent with Isaiah's portrait of the Babylonian king?
- He shows off his wealth by giving a banquet for 1,000 guests. This is the "pomp" described in Isaiah 14:11.
- We see the aggressive history of Babylon (Isaiah 14:3-6) in the fact that the king has objects looted from the temple in Jerusalem.
- Belshazzar decides to use the gold and silver goblets from God's temple to toast the Babylonian gods. With this act of disrespect he is raising himself and his nation above the true God—as he does in Isaiah 14:13-14.

How does Daniel interpret the situation?
Daniel reminds Belshazzar that his grandfather, Nebuchadnezzar, had made divine claims, and that God had stripped him of his sanity (v 18-20). For several years he lived like a beast, until eventually he acknowledged that God is God (v 21). Daniel warns Belshazzar that he has not learned from this but set himself up against God (v 22-23). The result will be his downfall (v 24-28).

5. Who else does God's judgment apply to? This is not just a plan concerning Babylon and the Israelites. Nor is it just for the Assyrians, Philistines and the other nations mentioned in this sequence of chapters. It is a plan for the whole world (v 26). It points to the judgment of all humanity. God is inviting us to look across history, see how empires have fallen and realise that these are all pointers to a greater and more terrible day of judgment when we will all give an account before God.

• **What is the hope given in verse 32?** There is a refuge from God's judgment. Zion was the hill upon which Jerusalem was built. But Isaiah is not talking about physical Jerusalem (since in chapter 22 Jerusalem is included in the nations that will be judged). He is talking about the people of God, the faithful remnant, those who find refuge in Jesus Christ.

6. These prophecies were spoken to the people of Judah, not to the nations themselves. How do you think Isaiah wants them to respond? Isaiah is showing that, in reality, all the nations they fear are under God's control. Whatever God plans will happen (v 24, 27). So they should put their trust in him.
This is also a warning. They should learn from the example of Babylon and humble themselves before God rather than seeking their own glory. After all, they too will die.

7. APPLY: In what ways do we get sucked into thinking that human glory and status are what matters? Why is this so tempting? We idolise wealthy, powerful and beautiful individuals. We listen to their opinions and want to know about their lives. We want to be like them and have the things that they have. Alternatively, we fear powerful people

and worry about what they will do next. But these are all ways of falling into the same trap which the king of Babylon fell into. We are putting humans above God. Perhaps this is because we are not content to reflect God's glory and instead want to establish our own. Perhaps it is because we do not really believe that God is more glorious than humans.

• **What attitude should we have instead?** The message of Isaiah 14 is that human glory is fleeting and temporary. Sanity is believing that God is God and we are human; believing that our lives are not in our own hands, but in his hands. Of course we affect the course of our lives. We are not mere puppets with no initiative, agency or responsibility. But we cannot really control everything and eliminate risk. We must recognise that God is in control.

8. Verse 22 says God will strike Egypt with a plague. God did that before the exodus. Egypt is an old enemy. But what is the new and surprising thing that Isaiah adds? God will not only strike the Egyptians but also "heal them". Like the Israelites at the start of the book of Exodus (Exodus 2:23-25; 3:7-9), the Egyptians will cry out to God and he will hear.

9. How will the Egyptians relate to God when this happens (v 19-21)? The Egyptians are going to acknowledge God and worship him with sacrifices. They will be faithful followers, keeping their promises to him.

10. What is God's ultimate plan for the Egyptians, Assyrians and Israelites (v 23-25)? Isaiah describes a highway (v 23). A highway carrying God's people home from exile is a common theme in Isaiah. But here it is Egypt and Assyria, Israel's great enemies, who travel on this highway so that they might worship God together. The outrageous climax comes with God blessing Israel, Egypt and Assyria equally (v 24). The language of "my people", "my handiwork", "my inheritance"—which previously has always been used to mark out Israel as God's chosen people—is now used to embrace God's enemies. It is hard to imagine how Isaiah could have proclaimed "Egypt my people" or "Assyria my handiwork" without being arrested for sedition. Yet this is God's grace.

- **How is this a reversal of what we read in Isaiah 14?** The nations have been worshipping their own glory, but God predicts that one day they will all worship him. We saw destruction and judgment promised in Isaiah 14, but the ultimate result is not death but life and healing.

11. The troubles of human frailty which we saw in Isaiah 14 have not gone away. But what is Paul's perspective on those things? Paul knows that human glory rots away. He acknowledges that "we are wasting away" (v 16) and "what is seen is temporary" (v 18). But he is able to view human frailty as mere "light and momentary troubles", because he also describes a glory that does not rot away or tumble down. This is the glory of God and he shares it with us. All we need to do is "fix our eyes" on him. Look at your troubles in the light of Christ and what do you see? God easing our hearts out of the rubbish tip and showing us to eternal glory.

12. APPLY: We often spend time thinking or worrying about the future. How might the passages in today's study change our perspective on this?

- We easily get sucked into pursuing human glory and status. We value our careers and we save for the future. But like the king of Babylon, we will die. We cannot take wealth or human status beyond the grave. So we should think carefully about our priorities and make sure we are glorifying God, not ourselves.
- We may think about the future because we are afraid of what might happen. But it is clear that God is the one who is in control. We should ask for his help and trust him to look after us.
- Ultimately we can be confident that God has a glorious future prepared for us. One day people from every nation will worship God and we will be part of that number. Thinking about this promise will pull our hearts away from human glory and towards eternal glory.

4 Isaiah 28
GOD'S STRANGE WORK

THE BIG IDEA
God works in strange ways. Even when he seems absent, he is not. He can use suffering to bring good things. So when God's work in our lives seems incomprehensible, we must keep listening and obeying him.

SUMMARY
At this point in history, God's people were divided into two kingdoms: Israel or Ephraim, the northern kingdom, and Judah, the southern kingdom. Both were now in danger from the Assyrians.

Isaiah 28 is the first in a series of "woe sermons". Verse 1 describes Ephraim's beauty and pride. It's like a scene from a picture postcard. But it's about to be ruined (v 2). True strength is found with God (v 5-6). But the people prefer the visions of drunken prophets (v 7-8). They don't want to listen to God's word.

Verse 10 appears to be the equivalent of *blah, blah, blah*. This is what they say when Isaiah speaks. So God responds, "Very well then" (v 11). *Blah, blah, blah* is what they will hear: that is, the foreign words of an invading army.

All this is really a warning for Judah (v 14). Judah is now seeking an alliance with Egypt against the threat of Assyria. Like Israel, they are relying on human strength and wisdom instead of on God. Isaiah is calling them to learn the lessons of Israel's history.

Verse 15 is a parody of their claims. *We have entered into a covenant with Egypt,* they proclaim. *More like a covenant with death,* says Isaiah. Everything that they take refuge in will soon be swept away (v 17-18).

Yet God graciously sustains Judah. The destruction is God's "strange work" (v 21). He is not doing what his people want or expect, but he is at work to purify them and bring life. Verses 23-29 explain this by comparing God to a farmer working his land.

So what should we do when it feels like everything in which we take refuge is being swept away? In Isaiah 28 only one thing is left standing: "a precious cornerstone" (v 16). The New Testament says this cornerstone is Jesus (1 Peter 2:4-8). When everything else comes crashing down, the sure foundation is Jesus. God destroys so that he can build, and Jesus is the foundation and cornerstone of that building. What do you do when it feels like God has gone AWOL? You look to the cross: God's ultimate "strange work".

OPTIONAL EXTRA
Use some toy bricks to build a simple building. Ask the group to make a new building, but don't give them any new bricks. The point is that they need to destroy your building in order to build a new one. Or find images of beautiful buildings and ask what the first steps were in their construction. It was probably levelling the ground or destroying what was there before. Or watch a video of explosives being used in a quarry in order to extract materials for building or other manufacturing processes. These are illustrations of what we will see in Isaiah 28.

GUIDANCE FOR QUESTIONS

1. Have you ever experienced a time when something that was unpleasant or seemed to make no sense was actually used by God for good in some way? We have all experienced times when God seems to have gone AWOL—absent without leave. We know what we want God to do, but he's not doing it. But when we look back, we often find that God has used difficult things to build our faith or make us more fruitful. God has been at work, even if it was in a strange way.

2. In verses 1-4, how does Isaiah express Israel's (or Ephraim's) pride in themselves?

- Isaiah talks about a "wreath" or crown which expresses the pride of the Israelites (v 1, 3)—it's as if they imagine themselves being crowned.

- Twice Isaiah describes "his glorious beauty, set on the head of a fertile valley" (28:1, 4). It's like a scene from a picture postcard.

- **But why is that pride futile?** God is about to send the Assyrian army to rip through picture-postcard Israel like a hailstorm (v 2). The people of Israel are about to be plucked from their homes like ripe figs being plucked from a tree (v 4).

3. Verses 7-8 describe some of Israel's leaders. What are they like? The people listen to the visions of drunken prophets. Whether their drunkenness is literal or symbolic (as 29:9-12 suggests) doesn't really matter. The point is that they don't see clearly.

4. Verses 9-10 report their response. What do they think of Isaiah's message? Isaiah is quoting the people.

Verse 10 appears to be equivalent of *blah, blah, blah*. This is what they say when Isaiah speaks: *Who's he talking to? This is just for children. On and on he goes. Blah, blah, blah.* "Whatever!" we might say today.

5. How does God respond to this (v 11-13)? If the people say God's words are "blah, blah, blah", then "blah, blah, blah" is what they will hear: the foreign words of a foreign army. The language spoken on the streets of their towns will be Assyrian and it will be coming from the lips of an invading army. *How's your Assyrian?* Isaiah is saying, in effect, *because that's what you're going to be hearing.*

6. In verse 15 Isaiah parodies Judah's claims about its alliance with Egypt. What does he say is really going on? The quote in verse 15 is not literally what the people were saying; it's Isaiah's parody of their claims. *We have entered into a covenant with Egypt,* they proclaim. *More like a covenant with death,* says Isaiah. *We have made Pharaoh our refuge,* they proclaim. In effect Isaiah says, *What you really mean is, "We have made a lie our refuge".*

- **What will happen (v 17-19)?** Judah's false hopes of being protected from Assyria by Egypt will be swept away, and it is God himself who will do this. They will no longer be able to take refuge in lies (v 17) and their covenant with death will be annulled (v 18). As a result, the danger they scoffed at in verse 15 will beat them down (v 18-19).

7. APPLY: This passage functions as a warning to us, too. In what ways are we, even as Christians, tempted to act like Israel or Judah? Confronted with our sin, confronted with

God's judgment, confronted with our inadequacies, people take refuge in a lie. "We are basically good." "It's just the way I am." "It's in our DNA." Christians do this too. What the heart desires, the mind justifies. We find excuses for our sin. We minimise it. We pretend it's inevitable. We blame our circumstances. Or re-define sin. We talk about personality types or cultural differences. We talk about Christian freedom. We talk about being contemporary. We take refuge in a lie.

- **What can we learn from their story?** We must acknowledge God's standards of righteousness and justice (v 17). Then we will realise the truth that we are all found wanting. Our only hope is Christ. So we must repent of our sin and ask God to help us.

8. In verse 24 Isaiah describes the work of a farmer ploughing land. It is a violent process. But what is the farmer's ultimate purpose (v 25)? The farmer ploughs so that he can plant.

- **What does that tell us about God's purposes in allowing his people to suffer?** God's aim is to bring life. There may be times when it feels like God is ploughing up our hearts. But the result will be greater fruit.

9. In verses 27-28 Isaiah describes someone grinding spices and grain. What do these images suggest about the way God uses suffering? Just like a farmer using different tools for different crops, there is a proportionality about God's strange work. It is carefully measured. God allows us to suffer no more than is required to achieve his purpose in our lives.

EXPLORE MORE
Read Hebrews 12:7-11. How is hardship described here? It is fatherly discipline (v 7-9) or a training programme (v 11). **What is God's purpose in this?** God disciplines us for our good (v 10) to make us bear more fruit—"a harvest of righteousness and peace". **So how are we to respond when we suffer?** We are to "endure" hardship (v 7) and "submit" to our heavenly Father (v 9). This does not mean being passive all the time. Rather it means seeking God and his righteousness in every situation.

10. Back in verses 16-17, God describes a new building project which will stand amid all the destruction. What is it like? God has swept away all the lies and false strength on which the people have relied. Now he is building something that is "tested" and "sure" (v 16). Instead of falsehood and compromise, it will be characterised by justice and righteousness (v 17). It will all be based around a "precious cornerstone".
1 Peter 2:4-8 says this cornerstone is Jesus. God destroyed his people and let them be taken into exile so that he could build them afresh. The cornerstone and foundation of the new building is Christ.

11. The ultimate "strange work" of God is the cross. In what ways did that seem destructive? What good things did God bring about through it?
- The cross was an act of judgment that brought forgiveness.
- The cross was an act of abandonment that brought reconciliation.
- The cross was an act of shame that brought glory.
- The cross was an act of defeat that brought victory.

12. APPLY: In what ways are we tempted to "panic" (v 16)—getting in a flap and trying to solve our own problems instead of listening to God?

- We may be too busy because we are insecure and seek to control life instead of trusting God as our sovereign heavenly Father.
- We may fear other people and end up being unable to say no instead of remembering that God's opinion is the one that matters.
- We may fill our lives with activity in a desperate attempt to find satisfaction even though God is good and the true source of joy.
- We may try to prove ourselves through our work or ministry even though God is gracious and justifies us freely through faith in the finished work of Christ.

- **What difference will it make to remember that Christ is our cornerstone and that God is building us into a holy people?** In the midst of pain and confusion, it may seem as if God doesn't care. But when we look to the cross, we see the full extent of God's love. We may not be able to explain exactly how God is at work in every crisis that engulfs us. But we can trust that God is at work and that he is at work for our good. And if we can trust, we can begin to be at peace, with the help of the Holy Spirit.

5 Isaiah 37:1 – 38:20
DEFENDING GOD'S HONOUR

THE BIG IDEA
God is able to help and save us—and he does so for the sake of his own reputation and glory. So we can trust him and pray for his help because he really is far more powerful than anyone else and he wants people to realise that.

SUMMARY
We now turn from prophetic oracle to historical narrative. The Assyrian army has invaded Judah. An Assyrian commander has been speaking to the people, claiming that Sennacherib (the Assyrian leader) is more powerful than God. King Hezekiah sends messengers to Isaiah (v 1-4). He sees clearly that the issue is the Lord's reputation. God agrees (v 6).

There is a short lull as the Assyrian commander withdraws (v 8), but soon Sennacherib himself resumes the threat, sending a letter to Hezekiah (v 9-13). Hezekiah responds by spreading the letter out before God (v 14-20). Despite the powerful claims of the Assyrians, Hezekiah still has confidence in God. His description of who God is provides a list of reasons to think that Sennacherib's track record of victory over other nations counts for nothing when he confronts the God of Israel.

Hezekiah draws God's attention to the way Sennacherib has dishonoured him. He is making a request for deliverance, but primarily it's a request for God to defend his honour and magnify his name.

So God promises failure for Sennacherib (v 21-29) and national renewal for Hezekiah (v 30-35). He will save Jerusalem (v 33-35). Again, the key issue is the fact that Sennacherib has insulted God. Sure enough, what Isaiah promised duly happens (v 36-38).

But Hezekiah now meets with fresh disaster: he becomes extremely ill and Isaiah advises him to prepare for death (38:1). Hezekiah, though, prays for deliverance with bitter tears and so God promises to add 15 extra years to his life (v 2-7). In verses 10-20 Hezekiah celebrates this recovery. He begins by describing the threat to his life posed by his illness in a powerful series of images depicting human frailty (v 10-14). Then he cites two reasons for his recovery. First, God has overlooked his sins (v 17). It is not because of his own faithfulness that he has recovered but because of God's.

Second, his recovery brings praise to God (v 18-20). For Hezekiah this is only temporary. But when those who are in Christ are raised to eternal life, we will praise God for ever. No one will ever be able to insult God again.

OPTIONAL EXTRA

Choose some famous faces and ask the group to vote on which one would help them in a given situation. Situations could include: you're marooned on a desert island; you need to help your daughter with her maths homework; you've fallen while hiking and broken your leg; you want to put up some shelves; you want someone to sing at your wedding. People may disagree on which famous person they would ask for help! But the point is that they would ask based on that person's reputation—in the same way that we

ask God for help because we know he is powerful to help us.

GUIDANCE FOR QUESTIONS

1. How do you decide if someone is trustworthy? Normally we trust people because we know something about them; we have had experience of them being trustworthy in the past. This can include someone whom you only know by reputation—for example, when a friend recommends a good plumber. This question introduces us to thinking about why we trust God and why his reputation is so important.

2. An Assyrian commander has been speaking to the people. How do Hezekiah (v 4) and God himself, through Isaiah (v 6), evaluate his words? Hezekiah sees clearly that the issue is the Lord's reputation. The commander aims to ridicule God. The Lord, too, recognises that his reputation is at stake, saying, "The underlings of the king of Assyria have blasphemed me".

EXPLORE MORE
Read Isaiah 36:4-20. How does he ridicule and blaspheme God in these speeches?
- v 7: The Assyrian commander says God's people cannot depend on God because Hezekiah has removed his "high places" and "altars". In fact these were religious shrines that God had forbidden and their removal had delighted him (2 Kings 18:5-6). But you can imagine how this claim might sow doubt in the minds of many in Jerusalem, especially those wary of Hezekiah's religious reforms.
- v 10: He claims to have divine sanction from the Lord to destroy Judah.
- v 14-15: Speaking directly to the people,

he tells them that Hezekiah is deceiving them when he says God will deliver them.

- v 18-20: He points out that just like Judah, other nations thought their gods would save them—but none has. His theology is clear: no god can stand against the power of the Assyrian military machine.

What does he say to represent Assyria as more powerful than God?

- v 8: He mockingly offers Judah 2,000 horses to even things up a bit—suggesting it is only with Assyrian help that they stand a chance.
- v 16-17: Promising a new golden age, he calls on the people of Jerusalem to put their faith in the peace promised by Sennacherib rather than to put their faith in the deliverance promised by the Lord.
- v 20: He directly compares Assyria's strength with all other gods, and by implication with the Lord.

3. What is Sennacherib's argument in verses 10-13? He cites the formidable track record of the Assyrian army, listing other nations whose gods failed to save them and other kings who have been defeated. Sennacherib's aim seems to be to increase the pressure on Hezekiah with the hope of wrapping up his Judaean campaign swiftly.

4. Look at the ways Hezekiah addresses God in verses 16-20. How does he describe God and why are those descriptions relevant to what Sennacherib has just said?

- Jerusalem's God is the "Lord Almighty" (v 16) and there are no limitations to his power. He is a greater king than Sennacherib.
- The Lord is "God over all the kingdoms of the earth" (v 16). When Sennacherib comes against Judah it is not Assyria's gods versus another nation's gods. It is

Sennacherib against the one, true God.

- The Lord is the one who "made heaven and earth" (v 16). By contrast, other gods are made. The gods of the nations are not gods at all, but the God of Israel is "the living God" (v 17).
- The Lord is "enthroned between the cherubim" (v 16). This is more than simply a claim that God in heaven is encircled by angels. This is a very specific location. The ark in the tabernacle and temple had two cherubim on top. Between the cherubim was "the atonement cover" (Exodus 35:12)—the place where atonement was made by the high priest on the Day of Atonement (Leviticus 16:15-16). So the point is that, while other gods only make demands, the Lord shows mercy.

5. What is Hezekiah asking God to do and why? Hezekiah invites God to take note of what's happening (v 17). Notice the five injunctions: "give ear … hear … open your eyes … see … listen". Hezekiah is drawing God's attention to the situation. But the situation in question is not so much the plight of Jerusalem (though that is implicit) but the honour of God. This emphasis is reflected again in the climax of the prayer as Hezekiah makes his core request in verse 20. It's a request for deliverance, but primarily it's a request for God to defend his honour and magnify his name.

6. APPLY: How often is the glory and reputation of God's name the key issue that is at stake in our own prayers? How would it change our prayers if it were more central?

- Sometimes our prayers can be a bit like running through a checklist. But Hezekiah gives us a model for "arguing" with God in prayer. Of course, we can't manipulate God. But we can present arguments to

God based on what he is like. This can make our prayer life deeper and more heartfelt: it gives us more to say to God. It also means we are likely to pray more biblical prayers which are in line with what God is like and what he wants to do in each situation.

- Praying for the glory of God also means praying more missionary prayers. What Hezekiah wants is for the nations to know God as Hezekiah knows him (v 20). The best way to pray for the glory of God is to pray for the mission of the church. And the best argument when we pray for the mission of the church is the glory of God. We pray for people to turn from the rejection of God to the worship of God.

If you have time, now would be a good time to pause to pray together, putting your ideas into practice. You could try asking each person to write out a prayer—it could be about anything at all, but God's reputation should be central.

7. What is God's message in…

- **verses 22-27?** Sennacherib has ridiculed the Lord and claimed to ascend the heights of the geopolitical stage through his own power. But in reality he is simply a tool in God's hands.

- **verses 28-29?** Now, because Sennacherib has failed to honour God, he will get a taste of his own medicine.

- **verses 30-32?** God then promises national renewal to Hezekiah. The economy will recover and a faithful remnant of God's people will emerge. It's a promise for the next three years (v 30), but the promise of the remnant will take on renewed significance when God's people find themselves in Babylonian exile.

- **verses 33-35?** Finally, God promises to save Jerusalem. This is "for the sake of

David my servant"—that is, to fulfil his promise that one of David's sons would always reign over God's people (2 Samuel 7:15-16).

8. What is the key thing that Sennacherib has done wrong?

Sennacherib has dishonoured God in the way he has spoken about him. Specifically, he has ridiculed, blasphemed, raged and been insolent against the Lord (v 23, 28-29).

9. How does Hezekiah describe what had happened to him (v 10-14)?

Hezekiah describes the threat to his life posed by his illness in a powerful series of images depicting human frailty. His life is like a tent being pulled down (v 12) or a piece of fabric being rolled up or cut off (v 12); he is like a watchman being attacked by a lion (v 13) or a mourning bird (v 14).

- **How does God fit into this portrayal?** Hezekiah doesn't want to die because he longs to continue seeing God at work among the living (v 11). He sees God as the cause of his impending death ("he has cut me off", v 12; "you made an end of me", v 12, 13; "he broke all my bones", v 13) and also as the only possible source of deliverance (v 14).

10. What reasons for his recovery does Hezekiah identify (v 15-20)?

- v 15-16: Hezekiah celebrates his restoration by acknowledging that it comes from God (v 15-16).
- v 17: Hezekiah receives life instead of death because God has overlooked his sins. In Hezekiah's case this is a temporary measure, but it points to the cross, where sin was ultimately paid for, leading to eternal life for all who belong to Christ.
- v 18-20: Hezekiah's recovery brings praise to God. Only the living can sing his

praises. Again, in Hezekiah's case this is only temporary. But when those who are in Christ are raised to eternal life, we will praise God for ever. Hezekiah's passion for God's glory will extend into coming ages.

11. What parallels are there between Hezekiah's illness in chapter 38 and the predicament of God's people in chapter 37?
- Both stories involve seemingly inevitable destruction which is averted solely by the intervention of God.
- There is a concern for God's reputation in both stories. Hezekiah asks God to deliver his people on the basis of his own glory. Similarly, when Hezekiah himself is delivered, he acknowledges that it is God who has done it and promises to praise him.

12. APPLY: How can you get better at trusting and praising God in all situations? Why is this so important?
We need to keep reminding ourselves who God is, and we need to keep coming back to his word. This is what will calm our hearts in times of crisis and correct our perspective when we crave acceptance or fear rejection. It is also what will help us to keep praising God—which will itself help to transform our hearts and minds. This is important not only for our own well-being but also because God deserves praise. If we trust God and talk about how trustworthy he is, others are more likely in turn to see the difference he makes in our lives and turn to him as a result—bringing him still more praise and glory.

6 Isaiah 40
COMFORT MY PEOPLE

THE BIG IDEA
God comes to deliver his people. This is good news that we are called to share!

SUMMARY
Isaiah now looks forward 200 years. He is writing to refugees who had been dragged away into exile in Babylon. He writes with "comfort" (v 1) and good news: "Here is your God" (v 9)!

What Isaiah's readers face is not just a political crisis but a spiritual crisis: a crisis of faith. They may feel abandoned by God. But God knows what is happening and has come to rescue them. "The Sovereign LORD comes with power", says verse 10. This is summarising what Isaiah has said in verses 3-5. He hears a voice calling for a construction project: *raise the valleys, lower the hills, level the rough ground to make a flat, fast highway.* It's like a processional route being prepared for a powerful king coming to rule his people and bring them out of exile.

Verse 10 also says that God brings "reward" and "recompense". This refers back to verses 1-2, which also talk about reward and payment. Here the sin of God's people has been paid for and the punishment is complete.

Mark opens his Gospel by quoting Isaiah 40:3-5. The voice calling in the wilderness is the voice of John the Baptist. So the God who comes with power to rule is Jesus. God has come in the person of his Son to lead us home. Jesus has paid for our sin (v 2) by his death and given us the reward of eternal life.

That is good news! It's news worth shouting about. So Isaiah says, "Lift up your voice … do not be afraid" (v 9). Jesus is coming to gather his people (v 11)—and one of the ways he does that is as we proclaim the word.

After all, "the word of our God endures for ever" (v 8)—unlike anything else. Verses 12-26 powerfully express this supremacy by comparing God and human powers. The chapter concludes with an encouragement not to complain (v 27-31): God is on the throne and he will renew the strength of his people. We really do have good news to declare!

OPTIONAL EXTRA

Ask group members to watch in advance a clip of the "Comfort ye" section of Handel's *Messiah*, which is based on today's passage. How did they respond to it? What did they think about or feel as they listened?

GUIDANCE FOR QUESTIONS

1. In what situations might people today feel restless and rootless, like exiles? Some may feel rootless because they have experienced a change of job, a house move, or the end of a relationship. Or they may be restless because they are dissatisfied with life in some way. Of course, there are many people in the world who experience much greater levels of vulnerability. They may be forced to

leave their homes or even their country due to unrest, war or economic problems. This is the experience of Isaiah's audience in chapters 40 – 55. He is writing to refugees who have seen their homeland torn apart and been dragged away into exile.

2. Isaiah is given a message with which to comfort people. The heart of this message is in verse 9. What is it? "Here is your God."

- **Why might this be comforting—and why might it not be?** The people Isaiah is addressing are likely to feel abandoned by God. But God knows what is happening and has come to rescue them. To those who have preferred to live life without God, however, this may come as a message of warning. God is coming and he sees all their wrongdoing.

3. Verse 10 says that "the Sovereign LORD comes with power". How is this illustrated in verses 3-5? Isaiah hears a voice calling for a construction project: *raise the valleys, lower the hills, level the rough ground to make a flat, fast highway.* Who travels along this highway? It's God. God is coming to rescue his people and reveal his glory. It's like a processional route being prepared for a powerful king coming to rule his people.

4. How do the promises in verse 10 contrast with what the exiles have experienced so far (v 2)? Previously they have experienced "hard service" and punishment for sin (v 2). But now God is sharing "reward" and "recompense" with his people (v 10). His arm brings power and strong rule instead of punishment and rejection.

- **Why is the time of punishment and exile over, according to verse 2?** Verse 2 says that the sin of God's people has been paid for and the punishment is complete. ("Double" here doesn't mean God has demanded twice what is owed. That would be unjust and cruel, and God is neither. It's more the idea of matching. The debt has its double—it has been matched by the payment that is made.) In one sense this is because God said Israel would spend 70 years in exile and those 70 years have come to an end. But 70 years could not really pay the price of sin. Human beings can never repay the debt we owe to God. Only Jesus could do that on the cross. The reason Isaiah can speak comfort to the exiles is that God is ultimately coming in the person of his Son to pay the price of sin. So the "reward" of verse 10 is actually the reward of life which Jesus won at the cross and which he shares with us.

5. In verse 11, what does Isaiah say God does when he comes? God tends, he gathers, he carries, he leads. God's arm is no longer a picture of power (as it was in verse 10). It's a picture of tenderness and care.

6. What did all this mean to those who were in exile in Babylon? God was coming to rescue them. The exile would come to an end (v 2) and God would replace Babylonian rule with divine rule (v 3-5, 9-11).

- **How was it fulfilled in Jesus' time?**
  - Sin has been paid for (v 2) because Jesus died on the cross.
  - John the Baptist came to "prepare the way" (v 3; see Mark 1:3) for Jesus.
  - This means the Sovereign LORD coming to his people is Jesus. The God who

comes with power to rule is Jesus. The God who comes to rescue his people and reveal his glory is Jesus.
- Jesus brings the "reward" (v 10) which he won at the cross and now shares with us: eternal life.
- Jesus described himself as the good shepherd (John 10:11). He now gathers his people through the mission of the church.

7. APPLY: Why is this message still relevant for people today? What might you want to say to people who are...
- **feeling guilt and shame?** We have good news of "comfort" (v 1): Jesus has come and has wiped the slate clean for all those who follow him.

- **facing the consequences of their sin?** We have good news—not only that the ultimate price is paid but also that through the work of the Holy Spirit we can be made new. There is hope for the future and there is no need to hide the past. Jesus himself said: "Blessed are those who mourn" (Matthew 5:4). In other words, blessed are those who feel the weight of their sin and who grieve the way they've treated God. Blessed are those who don't hide their sin or excuse their sin but confess it to God in repentance and faith. Jesus continues: "Blessed are those who mourn, for they will be comforted."

- **feeling abandoned?** We have good news that God has come in the person of Jesus. He has not forgotten us, nor will he ever leave us. "He tends his flock like a shepherd: he gathers the lambs in his arms and carries them close to his heart" (v 11). Jesus says, "I am with you always" (Matthew 28:20).

- **feeling frail or afraid?** We have good news that "the word of our God endures for ever" (v 8). Humans are frail and weak—like grass that withers and flowers that fall. But we can put our trust in the one who is eternal and who has promised to give us everlasting life.

8. As well as being the recipients of this message, we can also put ourselves in the shoes of Isaiah. What does God repeatedly tell him to do? God sends Isaiah out to share the good news. He is to "speak tenderly" and "proclaim" (v 2), "cry out" (v 6), "lift up [his] voice" (v 9), and so on.

9. What do verses 6-8 tell us about the nature of God's message? Human achievements come and go. Kingdoms rise and kingdoms fall. But God's word endures to this day.

EXPLORE MORE
Read 1 Peter 1:23-25. What is the effect of God's word on those who hear and receive it? We have been "born again" (v 23). Peter's point is that what God does in us is enduring because his word is enduring. We have been born again with imperishable seed—imperishable DNA, we might say today—because that seed was planted in us through the imperishable word.

10. What comparisons does Isaiah make in verses 12-26?
- v 12-14: First Isaiah asks questions to show that no one is really comparable to God. "Who has measured the waters in the hollow of his hand?" he asks. Who else but God! If you pour water into your hand you can hold a spoonful or so of water in your palm. But God can hold whole oceans in the palm of his hand.
- v 15-17: Next Isaiah makes an explicit

comparison between God and the nations. Before God "the nations are like a drop in a bucket". It's actually a drop from a bucket. If you empty out a bucket of water, you'll find there are a few drops left at the bottom. That's what the kings of the earth are like in comparison with God.
- v 18-26: Isaiah compares God to false idols. These are made by humans and are so pathetic that a skilled worker has to be found to make one that won't topple over (v 20). But God "sits enthroned above the circle of the earth" (v 22). Rather than being made, he is the Maker of all things (v 22, 26).
- **Why are all these comparisons good news for God's people (v 27-31)?** God is on the throne and therefore his people have no reason to complain (v 27). God's power is limitless (v 28) and he himself will renew their strength (v 29-31).

11. Why is all this a motivation to lift up our voices?
- If other gods, nations and powers are as "nothing" before God (v 23), then he is the only one worth serving. If he tells us to lift up our voice and proclaim the good news, we should!
- This passage also helps us to trust that "the word of our God endures for ever" (v 8). God has already come in the person of Jesus Christ and will one day come again to rule. Our message is true and we can have confidence in it.
- We are "like grass" which withers (v 6-8). Without God we are destined for death. Life and strength come only from him (v 29-31). Our only hope is to "hope in the LORD" (v 31). That goes both for ourselves and for the people to whom we are proclaiming the message. They urgently need to hear it!

12. APPLY: How will you lift up your voice in the coming weeks? What will you say and to whom? You could split the group into pairs or threes to discuss specific people they would like to share the good news with. It may be helpful to encourage them to choose a particular verse or verses from Isaiah 40 to keep in their minds as they prepare to speak.

7

Isaiah 52:13 – 53:12
THE SUFFERING SERVANT

THE BIG IDEA
Because Jesus, the suffering Servant, took the punishment we deserved at the cross, we no longer need to feel crushed by guilt—although we do need to take our sin seriously.

SUMMARY
Isaiah has promised a coming Servant who would redeem God's people and become the light to the nations that Israel had failed to be. It is a promise fulfilled in Jesus. In this passage we discover how Jesus will redeem his people.

The main theme of 52:13 – 53:3 is the contempt in which the Servant of the Lord is held by humanity. In one sense, we have good reason to despise Jesus. He doesn't look magnificent or majestic. On the cross, he even looked less than human—his humanity had been stripped from him (52:14). It looked like he was being punished by God.

And he was—but this was not for his sins but for ours (53:4-8). The central idea here is substitution. The Servant dies in our place. Jesus endured God's wrath on our behalf. Our pain, suffering, transgressions, iniquities and punishment are all transferred to Jesus. And in exchange we receive peace and healing (v 5). Isaiah is talking about reconciliation with God. By nature we are God's enemies. But Christ has made peace between humanity and God.

The cross is not the end of the story. Verses 10-12 reveal that at the resurrection the Lord gives his verdict on Christ—and his verdict is vindication. It's not just Christ's innocence that is vindicated. His guilt, as it were, is vindicated. What I mean is this. Jesus died under the judgment of God. He died the death of a guilty person. He took our guilt upon himself and made it his own. He removed it from us and bore it himself. And now, through the resurrection, that act is vindicated. God confirms that Christ has borne our guilt in our place. Jesus is raised to a position of honour (v 12).

In the end, Jesus' reward is us: we are his glory, the display of what he has achieved. He cleanses and justifies many (52:15; 53:11). So every time someone is saved, the triumph of the death and resurrection of Jesus is confirmed once more.

OPTIONAL EXTRA

Divide the group into threes and ask them to create their own short sketches in which somebody takes the place of somebody else. They can be as creative as they like—the only rule is that they have to show both the reason for the swap and the result of it.

GUIDANCE TO QUESTIONS

1. Has anyone ever taken your place for something—either in a good way or a bad way? How did it feel? The aim of this question is to get the group thinking about the idea of substitution, which is central to today's passage and to understanding the work of Jesus.

2. How do people view the Servant (52:14, 53:1-3)? Why? The Servant of the Lord is held in contempt by humanity. People are "appalled at him" because of his "disfigured" appearance (52:14). He is unattractive and a sufferer, "Despised", "rejected", and "held … in low esteem" (53:2-3).

3. Why is the Servant punished (v 4-8)? How many different phrases describe this? The Servant dies in our place, stricken by God (v 4) on our behalf. He "took up our pain" (v 4), "bore our suffering" (v 4), "was pierced for our transgressions" (v 5), "was crushed for our iniquities" (v 5); our "punishment … was on him" (v 5) and "the Lord has laid on him the iniquity of us all" (v 6). "For the transgression of my people he was punished" (v 8).

- **Meanwhile what happens to "us" (v 5)?** "By his wounds we are healed". The Servant gets what guilty people deserve, while we get what he deserves.

4. Imagine a friend or family member were one of the people who "despised" the Servant (53:1-3). What would you say to them? The group may already realise that this passage is a pointer to Jesus and what he did on the cross. But don't allow them to talk about that yet! The point of this question is to get the group to see the strangeness of what is being described.

If a friend or family member were among those who rejected the innocent Servant, we might condemn them for not realising that he came from God. Or we might be more sympathetic—after all, there is "nothing in his appearance that we should desire him" (53:2). There doesn't seem to be anything special about him.

- **Or imagine a friend or family member were one of those who gain peace and healing through the Servant (53:4-5). What would you feel about the Servant's work?** Imagine that a friend facing serious punishment ended up walking free because someone else volunteered to take their place. Or imagine that a family member who had been sick for a long time were suddenly healed. We would probably be overwhelmed with relief and joy. These are the images which Isaiah uses to express what the Servant has done.

5. Isaiah is looking forward to the coming of Jesus. How was the description of the treatment of the Servant true of Jesus during his lifetime? Jesus claimed to be the Son of God, the Saviour of the world and the promised Messiah. But there was nothing in the physical appearance of Jesus that marked him out as special (53:2). If you had passed him in the street, you wouldn't have picked him out. He was a human being just like any of us, but we despised him for it (53:3).

Jesus' claims seemed especially mad as he hung on the cross. Whips pulled away his flesh until his bone was exposed. The crown of thorns sent trickles of blood down his face. His weakened frame collapsed under the weight of the cross. His face was harrowed by the inner anguish of his soul. As a result, he looked less than human—his humanity had been stripped from him (52:14). So he was despised. In Roman eyes his crucifixion marked him out as the very worst sort of criminal. In Jewish eyes he was cursed by God (Deuteronomy 21:23).

To anchor your discussions, it could be helpful to look up the description of Jesus' birth in Luke 2:1-7, his rejection in Nazareth in Luke 4:16-30, and his death in Luke 23:26-49.

- **How is it still true of him today?**
  Humanity continues to feel contempt towards Jesus. People may not reject Jesus the teacher or Jesus the moral example. But Jesus the Saviour who comes to rescue us and Jesus the Lord who comes to rule us is another matter. People "hide their faces" from him (53:3).

EXPLORE MORE
Read Leviticus 16:15-16, 20-22. What is the substitution here? One goat died as a substitute in the place of the people. Sin deserves death so this punishment was given to the goat as a sign that the people's sin was atoned for. The other goat was driven out into the desert as a sign that as a result of this sacrifice the sin of the people was being carried away over the horizon.

How do these goats point towards Jesus? Like the first goat, Jesus was

sacrificed on our behalf. As a result, our sin was removed from us—as with the second goat.

6. APPLY: How do we usually respond when we ourselves are rejected? How might this passage alter our perspective?

- Knowing that Jesus has endured this pain should help us to endure rejection too. After all, whatever rejection we experience is a pale shadow of the contempt Christ himself felt as he hung on the cross.

- Jesus experienced rejection because we ourselves deserve to be rejected by God. The weakness and shame that we see in him is our weakness and shame. So there is a sense in which we should not be surprised when people dislike or don't accept us. Our sin means that by nature we deserve rejection.

- At the same time, we should remember that as Christians we have not been rejected by God! Jesus offered himself, freely, willingly, for us, taking up our pain, bearing our suffering, crushed on our behalf, so that by his wounds we might be healed. We are utterly loved. This should give us a sense of security even when humans reject us.

- Peter applies this passage to suffering Christians in 1 Peter 2:20-25. You could have a look at that passage to help you answer this question.

7. How does the Servant behave through his suffering (v 7, 9)? It is clear that the Servant is innocent (v 9). Yet he offered himself up freely—not opening his mouth to complain (v 7).

8. What happens to the Servant after he has suffered (v 10-12)? Why? The punishment ends and he gains life and prosperity. He is "raised and lifted up and highly exalted" (52:13). This means that Jesus has successfully borne the guilt of humanity. The resurrection of Jesus is the sign that the Father has accepted the sacrifice and that the punishment is over.

9. What is the result for sinners? We are justified (v 11) and receive peace (v 5). Jesus "will see his offspring" (v 10)—in other words he has brought life to many people. The Servant's reward is you and me: he has secured our salvation. Jesus invites us to share his victory.

10. Why is the willing participation of Jesus important to our understanding of the cross? Knowing this helps us to realise that what we see at the cross is pure love. Jesus offers himself, freely, willingly, for us, taking up our pain, bearing our suffering, crushed on our behalf, so that by his wounds we might be healed.

11. Look back at 52:15. How will the nations respond? Jesus will "sprinkle many nations"—which means he will cleanse them from sin. As a result kings will "shut their mouths" in amazement at his message. In Isaiah 6:10, we were told that Isaiah's message would be heard but not understood. But now that kicks into reverse. A day is coming, Isaiah says, when people who were not told will see and people who have not heard will understand—people like me and you.

• **How do we see this promise being fulfilled today?** Every day, through the preaching of his word, God comes to yet more people and finds them. This is why it should be our ambition to see Christ preached where he is not known, as Paul reminds us in Romans 15:20-21, where he quotes Isaiah 52:15.

EXPLORE MORE
Read Isaiah 57:15. How does this verse remind you of the description of God in Isaiah 6? Isaiah 6:1 describes him as "high and exalted"—exactly the same words as we find here—and the seraphim name him as "holy".
When we feel crushed by a sense of sin, how does this verse help? There is no need to hide your sin or pretend that you've got it all together. For God sees his Son, "crushed for our iniquities", and he says to us: "I live … with the one who is contrite and lowly in spirit".

12. APPLY: What attitude towards our own sin does Isaiah 52:13 – 53:12 teach us to have? Standing before the cross is like standing in a hall of mirrors where you're made to look fatter or thinner, or turned upside down. The difference is that the cross reflects back an image of our true selves. It turns the way we perceive ourselves upside-down. If we think we're high and mighty—confident in ourselves and convinced we are doing a great job—the cross exposes our desperate need. We must take our sin seriously: we have all rejected Jesus and it is for our sins that he was crucified. But if we feel crushed and lowly, the cross lifts us up into the very presence of God. We do not need to feel overwhelmed by guilt. We are given peace and everlasting life.

• **What difference should that make to us day to day?** We can be patient and humble because we know we don't deserve honour or status. We can reject feelings of anxiety or inadequacy because we know that God loves us and is looking after us. We can forgive because we know we have been forgiven. We should also respond with amazement and praise at the message of the cross, and seek to share the message as widely as we can.

The list could go on! Encourage each person to think about what specific difference this passage will make to them this week.

8 Isaiah 60
LIGHT TO THE WORLD

THE BIG IDEA
God is light in the darkness, and he sends us into the world to reflect his light to the whole world. We ought to be communities of justice who proclaim Christ—knowing that, ultimately, people from every nation will be gathered in God's heavenly Jerusalem.

SUMMARY
"Darkness covers the earth" (Isaiah 60:2). Humanity is groping in the dark, looking for answers. And in that darkness evil breeds, creating a night-time of fear. But Jesus comes into the world and light bursts into our darkness. "Your light has come," says verse 1.

But the community of Jesus is also the light of the world. Light shines on us and as a result we light up! We "shine" (v 1) and are "radiant" (v 5), reflecting the glory of Jesus. We hear the gospel and our lives light up with joy. We become enthusiasts and enthusiasts radiate their enthusiasm.

Jesus calls his disciples to be the light of the world (Matthew 5:14). We are the fulfilment of Isaiah's vision. He describes people flooding in from many nations to worship God (Isaiah 60:6-9). The nations come to Jerusalem to discover God's

ways. But they don't come to geographic Jerusalem; they come to spiritual Jerusalem—to the church scattered across the globe. So we are to walk in the light and shine with the light of God. We are to proclaim Christ in all we do and say.

It's all so exciting. But Isaiah keeps on going. There's no stopping him. There'll be so much light, he says, we won't even need the sun (v 19)!

Isaiah is not getting carried away with his rhetoric. He sees the future: the new Jerusalem, the ultimate gathering of God's people. Isaiah describes the world's wealth being brought to God's people to build God's city (v 5-14). Revelation 21:24-26, John's vision of the new creation, picks up this idea. All that is good in the economies and cultures of the nations will find a place in the new Jerusalem.

You and I are called to be a light to the nations—in our homes, our workplaces and our neighbourhoods. This is where it leads. One day our witness will result in a city of light with people from every nation.

OPTIONAL EXTRA
Here is an activity about darkness, light and reflecting light. You need a candle, matches and as many mirrors as possible.

Give each group member a mirror and tell them to put them on the floor. Turn all the lights off in the room so that it is as dark as possible. Then light a candle. One by one, ask the group members to pick up the mirrors and turn them towards the light. Experiment with bringing the mirrors closer and further away from the candle. Then try turning some of the mirrors towards each other. What happens? Can you work out how to create the maximum number of reflected flames?

GUIDANCE TO QUESTIONS

1. In what specific ways does the world seem dark at the moment? What might it look like for light to shine? Don't let the group go straight to the "right answer" of sin and the need for the gospel. Encourage them to be specific about the effects of sin they see in the world. You may think of political or socio-economic issues in your own country or around the world. Or you may think of more local or personal problems such as illness, bereavement, unemployment or broken relationships. Difficulties like these can bring distress, unhappiness and despair. We need light to shine: hope of change, a resolution to conflict, new ideas and understanding, or simply a way out of an impossible situation.

Ultimately, of course, the greatest source of darkness is humanity's rebellion against God. We see spiritual darkness wherever we look: people who do not know the Lord and do not walk in his way. We long for the light of the gospel to shine in the hearts of those around us.

2. What do darkness and light represent in each of these verses?
- 8:21-22: The people curse God and as a result see only distress and gloom.

Without God there's no justice and no hope.
- 9:1-3: People are living in the "distress" of darkness (v 1) but will see the "light" of hope and joy (v 2).
- 42:5-7: Darkness represents captivity and blindness (v 7) but God's Servant (Jesus) will be a light for the world, bringing freedom and enabling people to see things the way they really are.
- 49:6: Here light represents salvation, which reaches to the ends of the earth.
- 53:11: Here light represents life.

3. What do you think verses 1-2 are talking about? What is Isaiah predicting? The light that has come is the Lord himself. God is coming in the person of his Son to bring light. This is a promise about Jesus.

4. The light shines—but who else does (v 1, 5)? We do! We are told, "Arise, shine, for your light has come" (v 1). When we look on Jesus and see his work in the world, we will "be radiant" (v 5). Not only is Jesus the light of the world, but the community of Jesus is the light of the world. Light shines on us and as a result we light up! We reflect the glory of Jesus.

5. What is Jesus calling us to do in these verses, and why? This illustrates what it means to "shine". We shine by doing good deeds that bring glory to our Father. Walking in the light means living God's way and proclaiming Christ. Then many others will praise him too.

6. Back in Isaiah 60:3-9, what is the result of the shining of the people? Isaiah starts to list those who will come to God to worship him: "Nations ... kings ... sons ... daughters ... Midian and Ephah ...

all from Sheba … Kedar … Nebaioth … the islands … the ships of Tarshish". These are people and places from across the world that Isaiah knew.

• **What does this point to in the modern day?** Today, through the mission of the church, people from every nation are being drawn to Christ. They are becoming sons and daughters of God.

7. APPLY: What can your church do to radiate the light of Christ in your community? What roles do good deeds have in the mission of the church? Isaiah calls us to walk in the light of the Lord so that the ways of the Lord are made known to the nations. We do this both through the words we say and through the lives we live. "If you spend yourselves on behalf of the hungry and satisfy the needs of the oppressed, then your light will rise in the darkness" (58:10). Our churches are to be communities of justice and care. As we welcome refugees, care for the marginalised, provide debt counselling, look after the elderly, set up social enterprises, visit the sick and adopt children, light shines in the darkness. Ultimately this brings honour and praise to God (60:9). We are to live out the gospel we are preaching.

8. These verses describe a restored Jerusalem. Where will the beauty and wealth of the new city come from (v 10-14)? This is an inventory of the world's wealth being brought to God's people. Isaiah looks to the day when the trading wealth of the nations will be used not for selfish, proud human ends but for the glory of God and the enrichment of his people. All that is good in the economies and cultures of the nations will find a place in the new Jerusalem.

9. Who will be the ultimate source of glory (v 13, 19-20)? God is the one who brings all these glorious things into the temple to beautify it (v 13). More than that, he is himself the glory and light of the new Jerusalem (v 19). One day Jesus will light up all of creation with his glory: there'll be so much light, he says, we won't even need the sun!

EXPLORE MORE
Read 1 Kings 4:20-21 and 5:1-12. Where did Solomon's wealth come from? Money came to Solomon from kingdoms across the Middle East. He also made a treaty with Hiram of Tyre, a coastal kingdom not under Solomon's rule.
What was it used for? The first thing we are told that Solomon did with his wealth was to build the temple. This was a dwelling place for God. So it was a way of bringing worship to God.
What parallels can you find in Isaiah 60? "The wealth of the nations" comes into Jerusalem (where Solomon built his temple) (Isaiah 60:11). This wealth is used to adorn God's "sanctuary" or temple (v 13). Just like in Solomon's reign, there is peace and well-being (v 17).

10. In this passage, John describes his vision of the new Jerusalem. What parallels can you find between this passage and Isaiah 60?
• John says, "The city does not need the sun or the moon to shine on it, for the glory of God gives it light, and the Lamb is its lamp" (Revelation 21:23). That's what Isaiah said in 60:19-20.
• John says, "On no day will its gates ever be shut, for there will be no night there" (Revelation 21:25). This idea is taken from 60:11-12, where Isaiah said, "Your gates will always stand open, they will never be

shut, day or night".

- Isaiah 60:11 continues, "so that". There's a reason the gates are always open. It is "so that people may bring you the wealth of the nations". And again John picks this up. He says, "The kings of the earth will bring their splendour into it" (Revelation 21:25).

11. APPLY: John's vision is a vision of the future. What will be the end result of the light we bring to our dark world? Isaiah is describing the mission of the church. But he's also describing the final glory of the church, when people from every nation will come to worship the Lord. You and I are called to be a light to the nations—in our homes, our workplaces and our neighbourhoods. Isaiah 60 and Revelation 21 describe the culmination of that witness. We should pray—and act—for its fulfilment.

- **Practically speaking, what can you do to reach different groups—whether in your community or further afield?** Perhaps you can think of ways in which your church's activities or outreach could be more accessible or appealing to people from different communities. The gospel transcends culture, but that doesn't mean that one culture can impose its norms on others or that individual cultural expressions are not valuable. God loves the diversity of cultures in the world and one day they will all contribute to the splendour of the new Jerusalem. You could also discuss ways to support cross-cultural missionary efforts—financially, through prayer, or through direct involvement.

12. APPLY: Read through Isaiah 60 again. What do you find most encouraging? What will this passage spur you on to do? One day our witness—your witness—will result in a city of light with people from every nation. Our contribution matters and the triumph of the gospel is certain. This certainty can fuel us to persevere in walking in the light and radiating God's glory.

13. APPLY: In our first study we read about a vision of God which defined Isaiah's ministry. How have these studies changed or enlarged your own view of God? What impact will you allow that to have on your life—and in what ways? It may be helpful to start by allowing the group to leaf back through the studies and remember all they have learned. Encourage everyone to share one thing which has struck them and what steps they will take (or have taken) as a result.

Dig Deeper into Isaiah with Tim Chester

ISAIAH FOR YOU

This expository guide by pastor and author Tim Chester is an accessible, digestible tour through the whole of Isaiah. Each chapter focuses on a key text and shows how its themes play out in the surrounding passages. It will enlarge your view of God and fuel your vision for the mission of the church. Written for Christians of every age and stage, this best-selling series takes a detailed look at the Bible in a readable, relevant way.

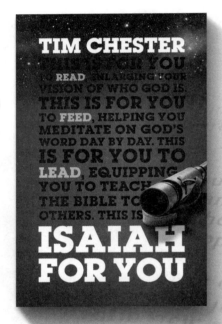

Isaiah For You is for you:

- *to read* as a book, mapping out the themes and challenges of Isaiah
- *to feed,* using it as a daily devotional, complete with helpful reflection questions
- *to lead,* equipping small-group leaders and Bible teachers and preachers to explain, illustrate and apply the Bible.

Find out more at:
thegoodbook.com/for-you
thegoodbook.co.uk/for-you

Explore Daily Devotional

These Bible studies help you open up the Scriptures and will encourage and equip you in your walk with God. Available as a book or as an app, *Explore* features Tim Chester's notes on Isaiah, alongside contributions from trusted Bible teachers including Mark Dever, Sam Allberry, Timothy Keller and Christopher Ash.

Good Book Guides
The full range

1 Corinthians:
8 Studies
Andrew Wilson
ISBN: 9781784986254

2 Corinthians:
7 Studies
Gary Millar
ISBN: 9781784983895

Galatians: 7 Studies
Timothy Keller
ISBN: 9781908762566

Ephesians: 10 Studies
Thabiti Anyabwile
ISBN: 9781907377099

Ephesians: 8 Studies
Richard Coekin
ISBN: 9781910307694

Philippians: 7 Studies
Steven J. Lawson
ISBN: 9781784981181

Colossians: 6 Studies
Mark Meynell
ISBN: 9781906334246

1 Thessalonians:
7 Studies
Mark Wallace
ISBN: 9781904889533

1&2 Timothy: 7 Studies
Phillip Jensen
ISBN: 9781784980191

Titus: 5 Studies
Tim Chester
ISBN: 9781909919631

Hebrews: 8 Studies
Justin Buzzard
ISBN: 9781906334420

Hebrews: 8 Studies
Michael J. Kruger
ISBN: 9781784986049

James: 6 Studies
Sam Allberry
ISBN: 9781910307816

1 Peter: 6 Studies
Juan R. Sanchez
ISBN: 9781784980177

1 John: 7 Studies
Nathan Buttery
ISBN: 9781904889953

Revelation: 7 Studies
Tim Chester
ISBN: 9781910307021

TOPICAL

Man of God: 10 Studies
Anthony Bewes & Sam
Allberry
ISBN: 9781904889977

Biblical Womanhood:
10 Studies
Sarah Collins
ISBN: 9781907377532

The Apostles' Creed:
10 Studies
Tim Chester
ISBN: 9781905564415

**Promises Kept: Bible
Overview:** 9 Studies
Carl Laferton
ISBN: 9781908317933

The Reformation Solas
6 Studies
Jason Helopoulos
ISBN: 9781784981501

Contentment: 6 Studies
Anne Woodcock
ISBN: 9781905564668

Women of Faith:
8 Studies
Mary Davis
ISBN: 9781904889526

Meeting Jesus: 8 Studies
Jenna Kavonic
ISBN: 9781905564460

Heaven: 6 Studies
Andy Telfer
ISBN: 9781909919457

Making Work Work:
8 Studies
Marcus Nodder
ISBN: 9781908762894

The Holy Spirit: 8 Studies
Pete & Anne Woodcock
ISBN: 9781905564217

Experiencing God:
6 Studies
Tim Chester
ISBN: 9781906334437

Real Prayer: 7 Studies
Anne Woodcock
ISBN: 9781910307595

Mission: 7 Studies
Alan Purser
ISBN: 9781784983628

the good book COMPANY

BIBLICAL | RELEVANT | ACCESSIBLE

At The Good Book Company, we are dedicated to helping Christians and local churches grow. We believe that God's growth process always starts with hearing clearly what he has said to us through his timeless word—the Bible.

Ever since we opened our doors in 1991, we have been striving to produce Bible-based resources that bring glory to God. We have grown to become an international provider of user-friendly resources to the Christian community, with believers of all backgrounds and denominations using our books, Bible studies, devotionals, evangelistic resources, and DVD-based courses.

We want to equip ordinary Christians to live for Christ day by day, and churches to grow in their knowledge of God, their love for one another, and the effectiveness of their outreach.

Call us for a discussion of your needs or visit one of our local websites for more information on the resources and services we provide.

Your friends at The Good Book Company

thegoodbook.com | thegoodbook.co.uk
thegoodbook.com.au | thegoodbook.co.nz
thegoodbook.co.in